Victorious Bible Curriculum

THE BEGINNING (PART 1 OF 9)

God created a home for mankind, and placed us in it to tend and guard it as His image. When we rebelled, God promised a seed of the woman to one day restore creation — and preserved that seed when our violence filled the world.

THE PATRIARCHS (PART 2 OF 9)

God chose Abraham to be the custodian of the line through which the promised redeemer would come. Abraham's grandson Jacob became the father of the twelve tribes of Israel, a nation that would bless the whole earth.

THE EXODUS (PART 3 OF 9)

For 400 years, God grew Jacob's tiny family into a nation. Through Moses, He released them from slavery to give them a new home. Despite the faithless first generation's rebellion, their children would inherit the promised land.

CONQUEST AND JUDGMENT (PART 4 OF 9)

Under Joshua, the children of the exodus conquered the promised land. After they settled in, they fell into idolatry and suffered under foreign domination. Time after time, they needed God's deliverance through a head-crushing judge.

THE KINGDOM OF ISRAEL (PART 5 OF 9)

God used Israel's first kings, the vacillating Saul and the head-crusher David, to give Israel peace. Solomon built a prosperous kingdom, which then split and fell into idolatry. After 70 years' exile in Babylon, God restored them to the land.

THE COMING OF THE MESSIAH (PART 6 OF 9)

The long wait for the serpent-crushing redeemer came to an end with the birth of Jesus of Nazareth. Raised in Galilee and baptized in the Jordan, He began to proclaim the kingdom of God and demonstrate God's love and power.

THE MINISTRY OF JESUS (PART 7 OF 9)

The blind could see, the sick were healed, the dead raised. The kingdom of God was truly at hand. But the leaders of Israel rejected the One God had sent to save them from their sins and deliver them into God's kingdom.

JESUS' FINAL DAYS (PART 8 OF 9)

On Thursday, before His arrest, Jesus ate one final meal with His disciples. Then He was arrested, beaten, falsely accused, tried, convicted and crucified. But death could not hold Him and the grave could not contain Him.

THE BEGINNING OF THE CHURCH (PART 9 OF 9)

After His resurrection, Jesus' followers received the power of the Holy Spirit to disciple the nations of the world, baptizing them and teaching them all that Jesus had said. Christ's body grew and began to crush the enemy's head under her feet.

Copyright © 2017 by Joe Anderson and Tim Nichols

All rights reserved
Printed in the United States of America
First Edition

No part of this book may be reproduced in any form or by any electronic or mechanical means, including information storage and retrieval systems, except for brief quotations in printed reviews, without the prior permission of the author.

Unless otherwise indicated, all Scripture quotations are taken from the New King James Version®. Copyright © 1982 by Thomas Nelson, Inc. Used by permission. All rights reserved.

Scripture quotations marked (NIV) are taken from the Holy Bible, New International Version®, NIV®. Copyright © 1973, 1978, 1984, 2011 by Biblica, Inc.™ Used by permission of Zondervan. All rights reserved worldwide. www.zondervan.com The "NIV" and "New International Version" are trademarks registered in the United States Patent and Trademark Office by Biblica, Inc.™

Author's translation or paraphrase indicated by an asterisk after the reference.

Illustrations by Gustave Doré
Colorized and modified by William Britton

Praise for Headwaters Bible Curriculum

These lessons are not just a way to teach the Bible to middle school kids. As I read the lessons, I found both my head and my heart irresistibly engaged. Joe and Tim have opened the grace and truth of God's Word in a way that seriously lifts us towards Christ while nudging us outward towards the world. I recommend these studies for both devotional and motivational reading!

Dave Cheadle, President of the Rocky Mountain Classis, Reformed Church of America

While I have spent quite a bit of time studying the Bible myself, I find your ideas and themes to be real food for thought and they help tie together much of the story God is telling throughout... I've already talked with people about your curriculum and have recommended they look into it for their own families. I can't loan out my copy for their perusal, because I'm using it everyday!

Linda Kidder, Home Educator, Colorado

I LOVE THIS BOOK!!!! We're just finishing up the Garden narrative. We've had such fruitful discussions—I have been pleased with it in every way. In fact, I'm hoping our church will start using it. I haven't had any problems or difficulties using the curriculum, I ONLY have good things to say about it. In fact, I'm in danger of writing in all caps I'm so enthusiastic about it.

Leah Robinson, Home Educator, Texas

I am really enjoying having this resource to work from and steer our lessons!

Christy Johnson, Bible Teacher, Bingham Academy, Ethiopia

Our family actually loves the curriculum. My children are in 5th and 8th grade and the content has suited both of their levels perfectly. To this point we hadn't found a curriculum that taught the Bible at such a detailed level that has also kept the kids engaged. We've had to slow down on the materials because otherwise they would be through them well before the school year is up. We are planning on buying the rest of the series.

Chris Turner, Home Educator, Colorado

How to Use This Book

This series of little manuals walks you through the biblical Story from end to end. Just read. Here are a few things you might want to keep in mind as you read through the Story.

- Try to love the characters. God does....
- The story is written in such a way as to make sin look stupid, but remember that the characters are all real people. No matter how stupid the choice, a real person actually looked at the options and then picked that particular one for reasons that seemed pretty good at the time. Nobody gets up in the morning and says, "I'm going to make stupid life choices that people will be mocking for centuries." Try to see it from their point of view. Ask yourself, "Why did this look like a good idea at the time?" That's how you learn to recognize temptations. It's easy to see sinful and stupid choices for what they are in hindsight, but in the moment it's often very hard. So learn to think through what these choices looked like from the inside, in the heat of the moment — you'll be amazed what you learn about yourself.
- Pay attention to the patterns. We'll point out a bunch of them as we go through the Story, but try to spot them yourself, too. If you can learn to read the Word and see the patterns in the Story, you will become able to read the world around you and see the patterns in the story God is telling right now.
- In the Old Testament curriculum, every lesson came with a Psalm. Not all of the New Testament lessons do, but you should know enough about how to connect the Psalms to the Story that you can discover your own connections. If there is no Psalm provided, feel free to take some time to read through a few Psalms and try to find one that fits. You'll be surprised what you can learn.
- As with any book that talks about Scripture, don't necessarily take our word for anything. Imagine you're sitting in a living room or around a campfire with us, and we're just talking about the Story. You're free to disagree, correct, challenge our understanding. The Word is the authority, not us — so grab your Bible and look things up yourself.

You'll find a section labeled "Activities" following the lesson. The point of this section is to immerse you as deeply in the Story as possible, through prayer, meditation on the Story, and other exercises. The "Evaluation" questions at the end of each lesson will help you to check your understanding of the material.

For Small Group Leaders
Have everyone in the group read the lesson ahead of time. Depending on how involved your group is, you can have them engage some or all of the activities, or you can save those for group time when you're together. The evaluation questions might serve as discussion starters if the conversation lags.

Table of Contents

Unit 3 Jesus' Popularity Grows 7
    Lesson 3.1 Galilean Preaching and the Call by the Sea 9
    Lesson 3.2 Jesus' Miracles Demonstrated that He is a Greater Priest 17
    Lesson 3.3 The Sermon on the Mount 23
    Lesson 3.4 Jesus Healed a Crippled Man in Jerusalem 31
    Lesson 3.5 Jesus Chose and Taught His Disciples 39

Unit 4 Jesus Rejected 47
    Lesson 4.1 The Turning Point: Galilee Rejected Jesus 49
    Lesson 4.2 The Parables of the Kingdom 59
    Lesson 4.3 Jesus Built His Disciples' Faith 67
    Lesson 4.4 Jesus Sent Out the Twelve Apostles 73
    Lesson 4.5 The Feeding of the 5,000 79
    Lesson 4.6 Miraculous Healings and the Feeding of the 4,000 87
    Lesson 4.7 The Leaven of the Pharisees 95
    Lesson 4.8 The Transfiguration: Peter Learned About the Path to Glory 101
    Lesson 4.9 Jesus Taught the Disciples About Greatness 109

UNIT 3: JESUS' POPULARITY GROWS

Jesus had been baptized, performed a miracle or two, and made a scene at the temple in Jerusalem. He was, what you might call, a person of interest. Word was beginning to spread that there was a new character on the stage, but Jesus' ministry didn't begin in earnest until He returned to His hometown and the surrounding region in Galilee. There He preached the gospel, cast out demons, healed diseases and announced the coming of the kingdom. After His hometown, Nazareth, rejected Him, Jesus moved to Capernaum where He began to gather disciples who would replace Him after He returned to the Father.

The parallels between the story of Jesus' birth and that of Samuel's indicate that Jesus is a new and greater priest from a greater priesthood. He called a leper clean, and His word healed the man. He declared a sinner forgiven and proved His power to do so by healing his paralysis. Both of these acts established that Jesus was greater than the priests in Jerusalem, thus offending the established religious authorities.

Ultimately, Jesus' ongoing contention with the religious leaders would lead to His death. In the meantime, He prepared His disciples to carry on after He ascended to the Father. Much of their training came from watching and imitating him. But He also spent some time directly teaching them. The Sermon on the Mount is Jesus' most significant recorded teaching session to His disciples. In this sermon, Jesus taught them how to relate to their good Father, how to relate to the Law, and how to pray, fast, give and trust God without worry, even in the face of great difficulty.

Jesus then went to Jerusalem and picked up where He had left off in His confrontation with the religious leaders. He did this by healing a disabled man on the Sabbath in order to demonstrate to the religious leaders who He was. This healing set the stage for a confrontation with the religious leaders who accused Jesus of working on the Sabbath. Jesus didn't argue with them; instead, He claimed that He worked on the Sabbath because His Father was at work too.

Jesus' disciples were starting to catch on, and they imitated Jesus by plucking grain on the Sabbath—therefore breaking one of the rules of the religious leaders. Jesus chose twelve disciples and called them apostles; these were the ones He was going to send out to do the same kinds of things He had done—miracles and all. After commissioning these twelve, Jesus healed a man from a distance and raised a widow's son from the dead—He was demonstrating to His disciples the kinds of things they were called to do!

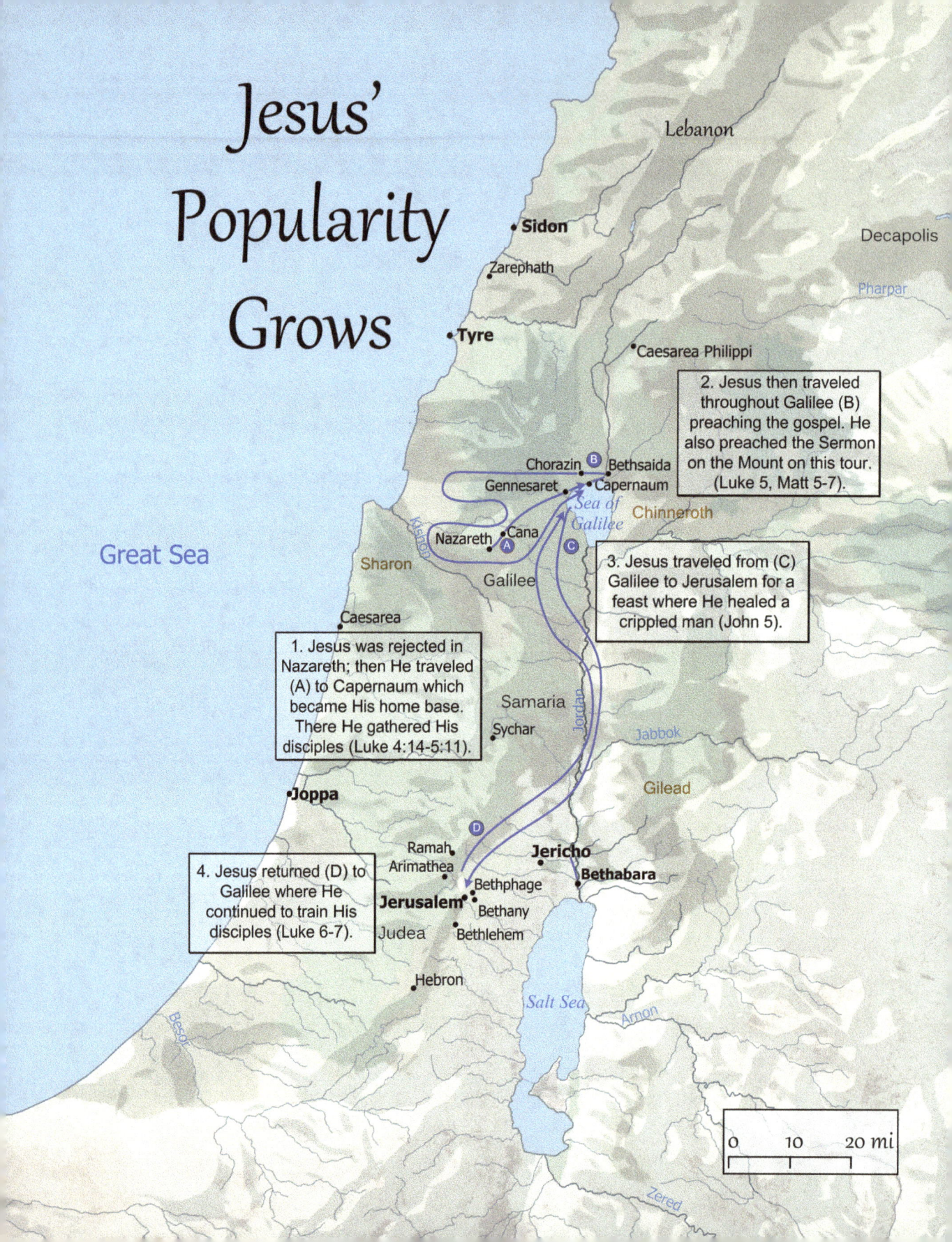

LESSON 3.1

Galilean Preaching and the Call by the Sea

UNIT 3

THE STORY

Lesson Theme - Jesus began His Galilean ministry with a bang.
Within minutes of announcing His mission in His hometown, Jesus was nearly thrown off a cliff. In contrast, Jesus was eagerly accepted in Capernaum where He cast out demons, healed the sick and preached the gospel, creating an enormous following in a very short amount of time. The main point here is that Jesus knew His calling and confidently began a ministry in Galilee.

Jesus grew up in Galilee (Nazareth); and though He was of Judean descent, He knew the Galileans, understood their culture and saw them, in their ordinariness, as the real beneficiaries of His ministry. Overall, the Galileans were a humble people, people of small villages and countrysides. They were not particularly wealthy or politically important; they were the *regular* people. Jesus' ministry lasted about three years, and a majority of it took place in Galilee.

In this lesson, we see Jesus' official launch of His Galilean ministry, but for several reasons, Jesus was already well-known in the region. First, Jesus was over 30 and He grew up in this region. He had attended and studied at the synagogue for many years and had garnered a reputation among the devout as being a faithful follower of God. He would regularly read the Old Testament and teach in the synagogue in Nazareth which meant that He would have been in a position of considerable influence (Luke 4:16). Furthermore, perhaps six months before, Jesus had turned water into wine in Cana and had performed some

OVERVIEW

Having returned by way of Samaria to Galilee, Jesus launched His Galilean ministry in earnest. Most of Jesus' ministry took place in Galilee where He preached the gospel, cast out demons, and healed diseases. He traveled from town to town, announcing deliverance and the coming of the kingdom everywhere He went. He began in His hometown, Nazareth, where He was rejected for not playing by their rules. He moved to Capernaum which became His home base. Jesus spent time in Capernaum, gathering disciples who would walk with Him throughout His earthly ministry.

SOURCE MATERIAL

- **Luke 4:14-5:11**
- Matthew 4:12-25, 8:14-17
- Mark 1:14-39

miracles in Capernaum (cf. John 2:12 with Luke 4:23). Word had spread, and He had a reputation as a miracle worker (Luke 4:23). Finally, many would have traveled to Judea for Passover when Jesus flipped tables in the temple and began His preaching ministry in the Judean countryside.

Jesus in Nazareth
Jesus began His Galilean ministry in an unassuming fashion in His hometown of Nazareth. On the Sabbath, He stood up and read the passage from the Prophets for the week (Luke 4:16). Jesus read a passage from Isaiah which speaks prophetically

Unit 3: Jesus' Popularity Grows

OBJECTIVES

Feel...

- surprised by the sharp contrast between how Jesus was rejected in Nazareth and loved in Capernaum.
- excited that Jesus performed so many miracles and brought so much freedom to Galilee.

Understand...

- that Jesus was already well known in Galilee.
- what Isaiah 61:1-2 generally says that Jesus' ministry was all about.
- why the people of Jesus' hometown rejected Him.
- that Capernaum became Jesus' home base for His Galilean ministry.
- which disciples Jesus gathered at Capernaum.
- that Jesus already had these disciples and was reconvening with them.
- that Jesus performed many miracles and cast out demons in Capernaum.

Apply this understanding by...

- evaluating your life to see where you desire Jesus because you desire life (like the people of Capernaum) and where you just want a pet Messiah (like the people of Nazareth).

about the coming of the Messiah. After Jesus finished reading the passage, He set the scroll down and returned to His seat (Luke 4:20). This was the custom; after returning to his seat, the one who read would explain the passage. What was unusual about this scene was that normally the reading would've continued to the end of the paragraph, but Jesus stopped in the middle of a sentence. As He returned to His seat, everyone would've been watching Him, waiting, and wondering what He was doing stopping at that point.

The passage Jesus read from (Isaiah 61:1-2) describes the ministry of the Messiah and says a number of things about His purpose (Luke 4:18-19). He was there to (1) preach the gospel, (2) heal the brokenhearted, (3) set captives free and (4) proclaim the acceptable year of the Lord. The Isaiah passage continues to talk about the darker aspects of the Messiah's ministry—that He would proclaim God's vengeance, but Jesus stopped before getting to that stuff.

When Jesus returned to His seat to explain the passage, He simply stated, "Today this Scripture is fulfilled in your hearing" (Luke 4:21). The whole of the Messiah's ministry included both good news and bad news; but at this point, Jesus was just there to do the good part.

This passage from Isaiah serves as a good summary of the ministry in Galilee that Jesus was just beginning. He would preach the gospel, heal diseases, deliver those tormented by demons and proclaim that the time of God's favor had come.

Jesus had become a celebrity in His hometown; "So all bore witness to Him, and marveled at the gracious words which proceeded out of His mouth" (Luke 4:22a). But Jesus wasn't there to be a celebrity, and He knew their true motives. When they said, "Is this not Joseph's son?" (Luke 4:22b), they were not expressing shock or disbelief; they were saying, in essence, "He is one of us, He is *our* Messiah." They were expecting that

a whirlwind of hometown miracles should follow. Jesus discerned their motives and immediately pushed back against them. The little proverb, "Physician, heal yourself" (Luke 4:23), simply meant, "Do for your own people what you have done for those in other towns." They wanted Jesus to make up a big batch of wine for His family and friends. But Jesus wasn't there to be His hometown's pet Messiah; He came to save the world.

Jesus gave them a firm rebuke and their response validated His read on their motives; they were angered *because* He had summed up their motives so succinctly. And, in their judgment, if He wasn't going to be their personal Messiah, He wasn't going to be anybody's Messiah. So they tried to kill Him by throwing Him off a cliff, but He slipped through their midst and went on His way (Luke 4:29-30).

In this little story, Nazareth represents Israel, and Capernaum represents the world. Jesus came to save the world, not to be a regional Messiah. So Jesus moved from Nazareth to Capernaum and set up a new home base (Matt 4:12-17, Luke 4:31).

Jesus accepted in Capernaum
Upon His arrival in Capernaum, Jesus did what He had done in Nazareth; He taught in the synagogue. In contrast to what happened in Nazareth, there is no report of a response of mixed motives; the people were *amazed*—and not because they were excited to get some miracles, but because His teaching came with authority (Luke 4:32). As a result, Jesus immediately began performing miracles, fulfilling the Isaiah prophecy He had read in Nazareth.

Before He had even left the synagogue in Capernaum, a demonized man yelled at Jesus, telling Him to leave and announcing that He was the "Holy One of God" (Luke 4:34). With Jesus' simple stern command to come out, the demon fled. After Jesus left the synagogue, He went to the home of Simon and healed Simon's mother-in-law (Luke 4:38-39). By evening, word had spread that Jesus was healing and casting out demons; numerous people gathered around Jesus, and He healed each one (Luke 4:40-41).

The disciples called
In Lesson 2.4, we learned that Jesus had already gained a following of disciples. His first two were disciples of John the Baptist who left him to follow Jesus. In addition to these, Jesus gained three more followers: Simon Peter, Nathaniel and Phillip. These five had spent some time with Jesus when He was in Judea (immediately after He was baptized); but at some point, they had gone their separate ways. When Jesus arrived in Capernaum, He was probably following up on a plan to reconvene with several of them.

Each of the three synoptic gospels (Matthew, Mark and Luke) record the calling of the first disciples by the Sea of Galilee; it's an important event. But it is not as though Jesus, through divine prompting, called men He had never met before to be His disciples. He knew these guys; Andrew, Peter and John were already followers of Jesus. Therefore, the call of the disciples recorded in Luke 5:1-11 represents a reconvening and a call to a more intimate ministry with Jesus.

Lesson 3.1

APPLICATION

At the beginning of His ministry, Jesus received a positive response in His hometown of Nazareth, but it turned out that they just wanted Him to perform some miracles so they could stand in awe and say, "That's our Messiah!" In Capernaum, people flocked to Jesus because they saw that He had something they needed: freedom from disease and demons and the freedom of the gospel.

Jesus came to *save* us, not to *impress us*. The gospel is *good news,* not a *good show.* The lesson here is that to know Jesus, to really experience what He has to offer, we have to approach Him out of a deep sense of hunger coming from a clear perception of our brokenness. Coming to Jesus for any other reason will *at best* get us an impotent Jesus of our own making.

Do you come to Jesus with that sense of need or for some other reason? If you lack that hunger, ask God for it; He gives generously to all without finding fault.

ACTIVITIES

1. Journal Time: Need for Jesus. In order to really experience what Jesus has to offer, we must recognize our deep need for Him. Spend some time writing in the space below, considering the following

Do you come to Jesus recognizing your need for Him or do you think He owes you something for some reason? _____
_____
_____
_____
_____

If you lack that sense of your own need for Jesus, ask God to help you recognize your need for Him; He gives generously to all without finding fault. _____
_____
_____
_____
_____
_____

Unit 3: Jesus' Popularity Grows

1. Loving like Jesus. Read Luke 4:18-21. List the things that Jesus said He came to do. Next to each item, list one passage where Jesus does what He said He came to do. You may draw from anywhere in the four Gospels. Lastly, list one way you might follow Jesus' example in your own life

What Jesus came to do	Example from the gospels	How you might follow Jesus

Lesson 3.1

EVALUATION

1. Was Jesus already a known figure in Galilee before He returned there to begin His ministry? How did people know of Him? _____
_____
_____
_____

2. According to the Old Testament passage that Jesus read in Nazareth, what was His ministry all about? _____
_____
_____

3. Why did the people of Nazareth reject Jesus? _____
_____
_____

4. Where did Jesus go after He was rejected in Nazareth? _____
_____

5. Which disciples did Jesus call in Capernaum? _____
_____

LESSON 3.2

Jesus' Miracles Demonstrated that He is a Greater Priest

UNIT 3

THE STORY

Lesson Theme - Jesus' miracles offended the Jewish leadership.

Jesus' Galilean ministry started in Capernaum, but what He did there was just the beginning. From Capernaum, He went from village to village in Galilee, preaching the gospel, healing diseases and setting people free from demons—just what the prophecy in Isaiah said He would do. But during all of this ministry, Jesus had a secondary aim; He was establishing Himself as a greater priest. He was declaring that His priesthood was greater than the Levitical priesthood, which would begin a confrontation between Himself and the Judean leadership. It was inevitable that Jesus would have to confront and undermine the entrenched and corrupt religious authorities in order to accomplish His mission. He had already started working toward that goal when He flipped over tables in the temple, and in this lesson we learn how the *kind* of healings He performed were also strategic toward His goal. Jesus didn't want to be in opposition to the Judean leadership simply because He was popular; He wanted to challenge the heart of their religiosity.

Healing the leper

Though Jesus performed numerous miracles during His first tour of Galilee, Luke recounts two specific ones, probably because of the challenge these miracles presented to the Judean leadership. (Remember, Luke is set up to show that Jesus is the new Samuel—a greater priest.) In the first miracle, Jesus healed a man with leprosy (Luke 5:12-14). After healing the man, Jesus instructed him not to tell anyone, but to go to the

OVERVIEW

Jesus is a new and greater priest from a greater priesthood. Instead of inspecting a leper to see if he was clean as the Law directed, Jesus declared the man clean while he was still leprous. The word of Jesus made the man clean. Likewise, Jesus declared a sinner forgiven without requiring him to offer the requisite sacrifices, and He proved His power to do so by healing the man of his paralysis. Both of these acts offended the established religious authorities, but that wasn't all. Following these miracles, Jesus went and partied with a tax collector without fear that He would dirty himself by doing so. Jesus is truly a greater priest.

SOURCE MATERIAL

- Luke 5:12-5:39
- Matthew 8:1-4, 9:1-17
- Mark 1:40-2:22

temple and offer the sacrifices required by the Old Testament Law.

Jesus was encouraging the man to do the right thing, but it was more than that. Under the Law, a priest would examine a person with leprosy and would pronounce him unclean if he was indeed leprous. After seven days, the person would be examined again, and if the leprosy was gone, the priest would pronounce him clean; then the person would offer the appropriate sacrifices. Jesus did the opposite: He examined

Unit 3: Jesus' Popularity Grows

OBJECTIVES

Feel...

- inspired by Jesus' compassion for the physically sick and broken.
- awe at the greater power of Jesus' priesthood.

Understand...

- that Jesus' miracles demonstrated that His priesthood is greater than the Levitical priesthood.
- that declaring the leper clean before he was cleansed of his leprosy and declaring the paralyzed man forgiven before he had made the appropriate sacrifices was contrary to priestly practice at the temple.
- that by cleansing and forgiving outside of the temple, Jesus was challenging the authority of the established religious leaders.
- that when Jesus ate with sinners, He was demonstrating that He could not be defiled by the sins of others.

Apply this understanding by...

- being a priest to those around you: pronouncing cleansing and forgiveness in the name of Jesus.
- not being afraid of being defiled by sinners, but being a source of life and light to them.

---

the leprous man, and when He saw that the man was indeed leprous, Jesus pronounced him clean. And immediately, the man was healed. Leprosy healings weren't common in Jesus' day, and this certainly would've provoked questions from the priests. When they asked, the man would've told them who healed him and how.

The claim that Jesus healed the man by pronouncing him clean would've been an affront to the authority of the priests: Jesus was claiming to be a better priest.

Healing the paralyzed man
Similarly, Jesus challenged the Pharisees and teachers of the law when He healed the paralyzed man (Luke 5:17-26). At first, instead of healing him, Jesus pronounced forgiveness: "Man, your sins are forgiven you," provoking the Pharisees and the teachers of the law to think Jesus was a blasphemer (Luke 5:20). Jesus knew what they were thinking and challenged it. Of course, when Jesus said, "Your sins are forgiven," no one could check to see if they were actually forgiven or if Jesus was simply making a false claim. So Jesus told the paralyzed man to get up and walk (Luke 5:24) to validate His claim that the man's sins were forgiven. Again, Jesus was making an authority claim to the Judean leadership in a way that they would get it. He was putting them in a position where they couldn't just write Him off as a charismatic speaker who could draw a crowd.

We read this story as though it was inevitable that the Judean leadership would reject Jesus, but He was giving them a real opportunity here. All they had to do was believe the claims He was making and lead the nation in repentance and following Jesus. Instead, they started to fume, which indicated that they got it... but simply refused to repent.

The party at Levi's house
In addition to using His miracles to make claims of authority to the Jewish leaders, Jesus used His interactions with people as a challenge and rebuke to these leaders. In rabbinic culture, each rabbi would have followers carefully selected from the best law-keepers in the land. Jesus

chose Levi, a tax collector (tax collectors were largely considered to be liars and cheats) to be one of His closest followers (Luke 5:27-28). In response, Levi threw a big party, a feast, and the house was filled with every shady character in town... and Jesus.

The Pharisees responded with indignation; they couldn't understand why Jesus would eat with these impure sinners. Jesus simply responded that He came for the sick, not the healthy; the sick were the ones in need of a doctor (Luke 5:32). Of course, the Pharisees and teachers of the law were the ones most in need of a doctor, but they wouldn't admit to it.

The Pharisees followed up their first question: "Why do You eat and drink with tax collectors and sinners?" (Luke 5:30) with another doozy: "Why do you eat and drink at all?" (Luke 5:33*). "Why do the disciples of John fast often and make prayers, and likewise those of the Pharisees, but Yours eat and drink?" (Luke 5:33). However, if they had believed Jesus' claims and knew who He was, they wouldn't have had to ask these questions. Rather, they would have known that the Savior was here and it was time to celebrate.

APPLICATION

Jesus is a greater priest. Instead of simply observing whether someone was cleansed of leprosy or not, He could make them clean with a word. He could forgive people with a word. And He wasn't afraid of being defiled by sinners; His presence among sinners sanctified them, rather than defiled Him. In a word, Jesus was more potent than the wickedness of the world.

We are priests in the line of Jesus and are called to perform these priestly duties in the world just like Jesus did: declaring the broken clean, pronouncing forgiveness in the name of Jesus, and not being afraid of being defiled by the sins of others, but being a source of life and light to those around us.

ACTIVITIES

1. Research Assignment. Research what a Jewish tax collector did in Jesus' day and why they were hated by the rest of the Jews.

Why would Jesus call a tax collector as a disciple? _____

_____

_____

Why do you suppose Matthew (Levi) was so eager to follow Jesus? _____

_____

_____

Unit 3: Jesus' Popularity Grows

What might have made Levi throw such a big party on that occasion? _____
_____
_____

2. Journal Time: A Greater Priesthood. Jesus is the beginning and head of a greater priesthood, a priesthood where the broken are declared clean, sins are forgiven, and life and light is shone to all around. We are priests in the line of Jesus and are called to perform these same priestly duties in the world just like Jesus did. Answer the following questions in your journal.

Is there someone in your life who needs to know that Jesus has the power to bring physical or emotional health? How can you pray for and encourage this person? _____
_____
_____
_____
_____

Is there someone in your life who needs to know that Jesus loves and forgives him? How can you share Christ's forgiveness with that person? _____
_____
_____
_____
_____

What are some ways you can be a source of life and light to those around you? _____
_____
_____
_____
_____
_____
_____

Lesson 3.2

EVALUATION

1. How did the manner in which Jesus pronounced the leper clean differ from how the priests at the temple did the same? _____
_____
_____

2. How did the healing of the man with leprosy present a claim of Jesus' authority to the priests? ____
_____
_____

3. How did the manner in which Jesus forgave the paralyzed man differ from how priests at the temple forgave? _____
_____

4. How did Jesus demonstrate that His forgiveness of the paralyzed man was genuine? _____
_____

5. What do the two miracles in Luke 5 (cleansing the leper and forgiving the paralyzed man) demonstrate about Jesus? _____
_____
_____

6. Why did the two miracles Jesus performed in Luke 5 (cleansing the leper and forgiving the paralyzed man) present a threat to the established religious authorities? _____
_____
_____
_____

7. How did the calling of Matthew and the feast that followed challenge the Jewish leaders? _____
_____
_____
_____
_____

LESSON 3.3

The Sermon on the Mount

UNIT 3

THE STORY

Lesson Theme - The Sermon on the Mount was Jesus' basic discipleship training material.
The Sermon on the Mount took place during the early part of Jesus' Galilean ministry and serves as an archetype of His discipleship training throughout this part of His ministry. At this point, Jesus only had several "close" disciples and hadn't yet chosen His twelve; but He had a large following of people who had seen His miracles and understood and believed His message. Many of these were committed followers of Jesus and we should rightly classify them as disciples even if they weren't in the inner ring. Later on, Jesus sent out not just the twelve, but the seventy-two, and those were chosen from a larger pool of disciples still. The point being, discipleship was the bread and butter of Jesus' ministry. Sure, He preached at times to hostile crowds and rebuked the religious leaders, but a lot of the time He taught vast numbers of hungry disciples.

Therefore, we should regard the Sermon on the Mount as Jesus' basic discipleship training material. Perhaps He preached the content over and over, highlighting different points in different venues; this was basic grist for His ministry. We should receive it as some of the most basic discipleship training for ourselves as Christians and for those we teach as well.

With that background in mind, there are two central ideas to grasp about the Sermon on the Mount. First, it represents the spoken portion of the whole aim of Jesus' Galilean ministry as recorded in Luke 4:18-19. Jesus was *proclaiming*

OVERVIEW

During His early Galilean ministry, Jesus preached the Sermon on the Mount, the archetypal sermon that Jesus would preach to His disciples during this part of His ministry. In this sermon, Jesus, the ultimate Son of God, taught God's many other sons how to relate to their *good* Father. Jesus taught Christians how to relate to the Law, how to pray, fast and give, encouraged them not to worry and promised that their good Father was eager to answer their prayers. He concluded with an explanation of how difficult being His disciple would be and included some signposts to look for along the way to know they remained on the path.

SOURCE MATERIAL

- Matthew 5:1-7:29

good news to the poor and freedom to prisoners; Jesus' discipleship training was deliverance for those in bondage. Second, the Sermon on the Mount taught disciples how to relate to God as a good and generous Father. Jesus, the ultimate Son, was teaching God's other sons how to relate to their good and glorious Father.

General commentary
The Sermon on the Mount begins with the Beatitudes (Matt 5:2-12). These short proverbs epitomize Jesus' mission to the poor and the meek as prophesied in Isaiah and recounted in Luke 4:18-19. As our Lord said in another place, He did not come for the well but for the sick

Unit 3: Jesus' Popularity Grows

OBJECTIVES

Feel...

- peace in knowing that God is a good Father.
- gratitude that Jesus gave such clear instructions on how to be a disciple.

Understand...

- that the Sermon on the Mount was Jesus' basic discipleship training material.
- that Jesus had lots of followers (disciples) at this point in His ministry.
- that the Beatitudes are not just prophecies of future blessing, but hope for here and now.
- how to relate to the Law as Christians.
- the importance of motives in giving, prayer and fasting.
- that God loves us and wants to provide for us: He is a good Father.
- some things we can do to get on and stay on the narrow path.

Apply this understanding by...

- evaluating your life in terms of the Sermon on the Mount and putting these teachings of Jesus into practice where you find weaknesses.

(Mark 2:17). Likewise, Jesus did not come for the rich but the poor; nor did He come for the free but the captives. There is a tendency to think of the Beatitudes *only* as heavenly rewards—if you are poor in spirit, you will be rich in heaven. But when Jesus talked about the "kingdom of heaven," He was talking about the kingdom of heaven *coming to earth*: "Thy kingdom come, Thy will be done on earth as it is in heaven" (Matt 6:10, KJV).

These blessings are blessings for now. Jesus wasn't announcing some sort of prophetic blessing once these people died and went to heaven. He was, at present, blessing the people He was speaking to... and He was blessing them because He was, at present, bringing about the world in which the Beatitudes were going to be true. He was bringing about a new creation, and that new creation held a new blessing for those who were prepared to receive it.

In Matthew 5:13-16, Jesus told His disciples that they were the salt of the earth and the light of the world. He was the leader of a new people, a people consisting of the poor and broken, the outcasts of the world; and these people were to be a city on a hill. These were the new sons of God, and their lives needed to reflect that new relationship so that the world would "see [their] good works and glorify [their] Father in heaven" (Matt 5:16).

In the next section of His sermon, Jesus interacted with the Law (Matt 5:17-48). The main point here being that He *was not* there to dump the Law. Rather, He was there to do it right... and teach His disciples to do the same. This new people that Jesus was forming was the new Israel and therefore was still bound by Old Testament precedents. However, by the time Jesus had come, the religious leaders had become strict moralists and treated the Law as a code to control outward behavior. Jesus pushed the Law back inside: it was about the heart. The command, "Thou shalt not murder," had *always* been about loving your neighbor, and all the outward conformity was useless unless the Law got inside and changed the believer.

Ultimately, the Law was aiming at bringing God's sons into conformity with their Father's likeness. In that day, rabbis would say, "Love your neighbor," as the Old Testament instructed, but added their own addendum, "but hate your enemies" (Matt 5:43). Jesus, however, told His disciples they were to love their enemies and pray for those who persecuted them (Matt 5:44). Why? Because God loved them, and that was the whole point of the Law: to be like God. God causes the sun to rise and the rain to fall on the righteous and unrighteous alike, and we should be perfect *as* (or in the same way) our heavenly Father is perfect (Matt 5:48).

In Matthew 6, Jesus addressed giving, prayer and fasting—three aspects of a relationship with the Father. Again, the Jewish leaders of that day had the whole thing upside down and backwards. They would give and fast and pray, not to develop their relationship with their Father, but to buttress their reputation. Their piety was public and therefore pointless. Jesus pointed His disciples back to the main point of these things: to please their Father. When we worship in the eyes of men, we forfeit the pleasure of our Father and in doing so, we forfeit our reward. Our giving, prayer and fasting should take place in private, because it is between us and our Father. If we do that, we are aligning ourselves with our Father's will and laying up treasures for ourselves in heaven, identifying more with His kingdom than with earthly satisfactions.

Children of the heavenly Father, Jesus said, need not worry (Matt 6:25-34). After all, generally, children don't worry about food. Their father provides for all of their needs and they don't even think about where it came from. If God is our *almighty* Father, what do we have to worry about? Furthermore, we are surrounded by evidence of His abundant goodness. If He provides clothes and food for flowers or birds, how much more will He provide for His children? Jesus completed this thought in Matthew 7:7-12—God is a *good* Father. Even fallen earthly fathers give their children good gifts when they ask for them; how much more will God give His children good things when they ask for them?

In the middle of this discussion of God's goodness, Jesus interjected a section about how brothers should treat each other (Matt 7:1-6). The Pharisees and teachers of the law had elevated hypocrisy and judgmentalism to an art form. Sons of the heavenly Father were to behave differently. "Judge not, that you be not judged," Jesus said (Matt 7:1). When everyone worries about other people's sins, and no one pays attention to their own, the whole thing is headed for disaster. On the other hand, it is good and right to *help* your brother when he has fallen down; but before you can help your brother out of the ditch, you have to pull yourself out of the pit.

Jesus concluded the Sermon on the Mount with a series of contrasts (Matt 7:13-27). He warned His followers that the path of discipleship would not be easy—"wide is the gate and broad is the way that leads to destruction... narrow is the gate and difficult is the way that leads to life..." (Matt 6:13-14). This was the first contrast Jesus gave and provided a framework for the other three. Part of the "wideness" of the road that leads to destruction is the fact that there are many false prophets out there eager to lead would-be disciples away. The good news here is that every false prophet inevitably exposes himself as a false prophet by his fruit. Those who enter that wide gate and follow a false prophet aren't actually disciples of Jesus. They may say the right things and even claim the name of Jesus, but in the end Jesus will say to them, "I never knew you; depart from Me, you who practice lawlessness!" (Matt 7:23).

In conclusion, Jesus implied that He was the *true* prophet. If you want to enter through the narrow gate, hear Jesus' words and put them into practice. The man who does that is like a builder who builds his house on a rock. Those who ignore Jesus' words will have their work come crashing down around them (Matt 7:24-27).

APPLICATION

There are lots of possible applications out of the Sermon on the Mount, many of which are sprinkled throughout the commentary above. What is the most relevant application to you? If you struggle with worry, spend some time applying Matthew 6:25-34. If you live in a highly religious environment, legalism and judgmentalism might be a temptation; if this is the case, focus on Matthew 5:17ff and 7:1-6. A number of application oriented questions are given in the activities.

ACTIVITIES

1. Who Are You in the Story? Jesus was surrounded by eager disciples, nominal followers, hostile crowds and antagonistic religious people. Imagine that you lived in Galilee during Jesus' time and consider where you would have fit into this story. Would you have been on that mountainside listening attentively to Jesus? Would you have been up close to Jesus or in the back row? Would you have thought all this excitement about Jesus was just hype and would have rather stayed home? Or would you have been an antagonist—only there to try to get some dirt on Jesus? Spend some time thinking about these questions and write your reflections below._____

_____
_____
_____
_____
_____

The Sermon on the Mount is a call to move closer to Jesus. Is Jesus asking you to move closer to Him? If Jesus is calling you to be a closer follower, tell that to Jesus: tell Him that you want what He has to offer. _____

_____
_____

Lesson 3.3

2. Jesus and the Law. Read Matthew 5:21-32, then write a short answer to each of the following questions regarding the Law. Be prepared to discuss your answers.

Jesus interpreted the Old Testament laws prohibiting murder, adultery and divorce. Does His explanations of these laws make them more difficult to keep or easier? _____
_____
_____
_____

With the command against murder, as it was normally interpreted, it was pretty easy to measure how you were doing: if you never killed a person, you hadn't broken it. How do you measure your progress under Jesus' interpretation of it? _____
_____
_____
_____

I thought Jesus was here to bring good news, but His interpretation of the Law sounds hopelessly impossible for those who want to know they are being good Christians. What's the deal?_____
_____
_____
_____

What can we do to find peace if we look inside ourselves and only find a sinner?_____
_____
_____

3. Personal Reflection. Reflect on the Sermon on the Mount and answer the questions below.

What kind of things do you tend to worry about? Do you think God cares about those things and wants to meet those needs? How can you know that God is going to provide in that area?_____
_____
_____
_____
_____

Unit 3: Jesus' Popularity Grows

Jesus said, "Judge not, that you be not judged" (Matt 7:1). Does this mean we should never point out someone else's sin? _____

_____

_____

What are we supposed to do before we help a brother out of a sin? _____

_____

_____

_____

Jesus said that it's easy to end up on the road to destruction and difficult to stay on the path of life. What does Jesus' discussion following this statement indicate that we can do to help keep us on the path? _____

_____

_____

_____

_____

_____

_____

Lesson 3.3

EVALUATION

1. What was Jesus trying to accomplish with the Sermon on the Mount? _____
_____
_____

2. Did Jesus have very many followers at this point? _____
_____

3. What are the Beatitudes all about? _____
_____
_____

4. Are the blessings of the Beatitudes for now or later? _____

5. Does Jesus make measurable obedience to the Law more difficult or easier? _____
_____
_____

6. Why is it a bad idea to pray and fast in order to gain the approval of others? _____
_____
_____

7. How can we know that God is going to meet our needs? _____
_____
_____

8. That whole narrow path thing makes the Christian life sound difficult; what are some things you can do to make sure you stay on the path? _____
_____
_____
_____
_____

LESSON 3.4

Jesus Healed a Crippled Man in Jerusalem

UNIT 3

THE STORY

Lesson Theme - Jesus confronted the religious leaders, claiming unity with the Father.

While His ministry in Galilee was in full force, Jesus took a break from that venue to go to Jerusalem for a feast (John 5:1), as many devout Jews from Galilee would have. In Jerusalem, He basically picked up where He had left off earlier that year.

Jesus' ministry in Jerusalem was almost pure confrontation; He kept miracles to a minimum and always performed them with a clear purpose. In Galilee, Jesus would interact with the Pharisees and teachers of the law as opportunity arose, but in Jerusalem, Jesus went after them offensively. Of course, His healing of the lame man was a real act of mercy and He truly did it out of compassion, but this passage is meant to primarily highlight Jesus' ongoing conflict with the Judean religious leaders.

Specifically, Jesus wanted to bring the leaders face-to-face with His identity as the Son of God—He wanted them to see that He was one with God. Furthermore, He wanted them to see His identity in a way that undermined their false religion.

Jesus made a number of trips to Jerusalem for the festivals, and normally John tells us which feast He was celebrating. John 5:1 tells us Jesus went to Jerusalem for a feast, but doesn't say which one. This appears to be something of a riddle; John is saying, "If you can figure out

OVERVIEW

Jesus went to Jerusalem and picked up where He had left off in His confrontation with the Pharisees, priests and teachers of the law. Jesus healed a disabled man on the Sabbath as a way to demonstrate to the religious leaders *who He was*. The man He healed had been in his condition for 38 years, just like the first generation wandered in the wilderness for 38 years. And like that generation, he lived in a temporary "house of grace" awaiting salvation. Jesus reenacted the deliverance of Israel when they entered the promised land by healing this man during the Feast of Tabernacles (or Booths). This healing set the stage for a confrontation with the religious leaders who accused Jesus of working on the Sabbath. Jesus didn't argue with them; He went along with it and claimed that He worked on the Sabbath because His Father was at work too. Elaborating on this, Jesus told them that they could expect a lot more from Him because the Father had given Him a lot to do.

SOURCE MATERIAL

- John 5:1-47

which feast this is, then you will unlock the passage."

Jesus came to a man dwelling under a covered colonnade, a tabernacle of sorts (John 5:2). He was sitting by the pool called Bethesda, which means "house of grace." He had been disabled

Unit 3: Jesus' Popularity Grows

OBJECTIVES

Feel...

- the compassion of Jesus as He healed a man who had been disabled so long.
- shocked at how Jesus responded to the religious leaders, pushing their buttons.

Understand...

- the clues that John gives that this healing happened during the Feast of Tabernacles and what that implied about Jesus' ministry.
- why sick and disabled people would gather at the Bethesda pool.
- that Jesus didn't argue with these religious leaders about working on the Sabbath; He agreed with them.
- what Jesus' purpose was in pushing the Pharisees' buttons regarding working on the Sabbath: to demonstrate His oneness with the Father.
- what Jesus told the Pharisees about His relationship with the Father.
- why Jesus' testimony of Himself (by itself) was invalid, and what the real testimony to the religious leaders was.

Apply this understanding by...

- evaluating your life to see if there is any ongoing sin that you can't let go of.
- asking yourself what Jesus asked the disabled man: "Do you really want to get well?"
- asking God to help you get well.

for 38 years... 38 years waiting in a home that wasn't his home, a "house of grace," yet receiving no grace. This is meant to remind us of the first generation of Israel that came out of Egypt and wandered in the wilderness in covered tents, "houses of grace," where God provided for their daily needs. Thirty-eight years they wandered there, receiving God's grace, and returning it with complaints until they began to defeat their enemies (in the last two years of their forty years in the wilderness, Israel began its conquest on the east side of the Jordan). One of Israel's feasts was a memorial of that time of wandering in tents: the Feast of Tabernacles, and so we have the answer to the riddle. This answer is further confirmed by the fact that the Feast of Tabernacles fits well in the chronology of Jesus' ministry.

There were occasions in Galilee when Jesus would heal everyone who came to Him with a disease or disability. This time, however, He healed only one man, even though the pool was surrounded by a great number of sick people.

The reason the sick and disabled would gather around this pool (according to John 5:4) was because an angel would stir it occasionally. When this happened, the first person to get into the water would be healed of whatever disease he had. This tells us something interesting about Israel at the time. From reading the gospels, we get the impression that Israel was under demonic oppression. Many were sick, paralyzed, disabled and demon-possessed. Graciously, God had permitted miracles like the stirring of this pool, and surely a great many people were healed in this way. On the other hand, it seems a bit out of proportion. There were a lot more sick people than could ever get healed by the stirring at this pool. Furthermore, Jesus came along and healed *only one man*. What was going on?

Look at the question that Jesus asked the invalid whom He healed, "Do you want to be made well?" (John 5:6). Like the first generation who died in the wilderness, many in Israel were in bondage to demons and disease and, somehow, didn't want to get well. They had chosen their fate; they lived in unbelief and remained enslaved. And when a city lacks faith, the healer passes over it. Jesus was there to free those of this unbelieving generation if they would only accept Him, and this man did. So Jesus told him, "Rise, take up your bed and walk" (John 5:8), and the man was healed.

This healing took place on the Sabbath, and according to the teachers of the law, carrying a mat broke one of the 39 Sabbath regulations. So they approached the man who had been healed to tell him that he was breaking the Law (John 5:10). The religious purists were so caught up in their rules that they didn't even rejoice that a man had been healed. Instead, when he told the religious leaders that the man who healed him had instructed him to carry his mat, they just wanted to know who was causing people to break the Sabbath... and breaking the Sabbath by healing (John 5:11-12). Jesus had slipped away and didn't tell the man who He was, so the man couldn't answer their question. But Jesus was aiming toward a confrontation with these leaders, so He found the man and told him to stop sinning so that something worse wouldn't happen to him. Immediately, the man went to the teachers of the law and told them who had healed him (John 5:14-15).

The Judean leaders were looking for an accusation to make against Jesus, and they found it when He advised this man to "work" on the Sabbath by carrying his mat. Not only was Jesus "working" on the Sabbath (by healing), but He was also encouraging others to "work."

We might expect Jesus to rebuke the religious leaders for misunderstanding the Sabbath—He set a man free who had been in bondage for 38 years—He was *giving rest* which was what the Sabbath was about all along. On occasions in His ministry Jesus made such a defense, but this time He played along; He answered the fools according to their folly.

In essence, Jesus said to the religious leaders, "Of course I was working on the Sabbath; My Father was working, as He always is, so why shouldn't I join in?" (John 5:17). He was trying to push their buttons and it worked, angering the religious leaders on a couple of levels. First, not only was Jesus "working" on the Sabbath, but He admitted to it! Second, He called God His *own* Father, therefore making Himself equal with God. The way Jesus worded it, saying "My Father" rather than "our Father" clearly excluded the religious leaders from the sonship He was talking about—Jesus was making the point that He had a relationship with God that they couldn't have; He was God's *only* Son.

As a side point here, think about what Jesus was doing. Our natural tendency when confronted is to try to make peace, find some common ground and have a discussion. Jesus only pushed back harder by saying that of course He was working on the Sabbath; He was just following *His* Father. Sometimes making peace is not the right thing to do.

Now the religious leaders *really* wanted to kill Him, but Jesus only pressed the point further. In John 5:19-30, Jesus elaborated on His relationship with the Father; He wanted them to *really* get what He was claiming. In essence, Jesus told them that He and the Father were so connected that He did *nothing* that the Father was not already doing. God gives life, so Jesus gave life;

Unit 3: Jesus' Popularity Grows

God raises the dead, so Jesus did as well. He had just given life to the legs of a man who couldn't walk, but Jesus told them that they hadn't even seen what He could really do. In fact, one day, He would raise *all* the dead to life—God had given Him the authority to judge the world, because He was the Son of Man.

The Son of Man was Jesus' most common way of referring to Himself. It was also a common term in Jesus' day. In Daniel 7, Daniel records a vision he had. In that vision, four beasts come out of the water, each representing empires that ruled over the earth. Each beast was worse than the previous. Finally, the beasts were defeated, and the Ancient of Days took away the dominion of each. Then, "One like the Son of Man" ascended to the Father riding on the clouds and received dominion over the entire earth (Dan 7:13). Jesus was given the authority to judge the world because He was this "Son of Man."

But Jesus doesn't judge the world independently. Just as Jesus only did what He saw the Father doing, He only judges as He hears from the Father, because He only seeks to please the Father, not Himself.

The religious leaders certainly got it. Jesus was making serious claims, and He was doing it in a way that they would understand, but they still had one possible objection. Here Jesus was making staggering claims about Himself, but what if He was just lying?

"If I bear witness of Myself, My witness is not true," Jesus said (John 5:31). People who claimed to be the Messiah were a dime a dozen during this time, so just saying things about Himself was never going to convince the religious leaders. John the Baptist, however, was in a much more believable position to give witness about Christ. He was on the scene *before* Jesus was and said that the Messiah was coming. He wasn't like every other wilderness preacher trying to create a following for himself. When Jesus came on the scene, John pointed Him out and, over time, receded into the background. This should've gotten the religious leaders' attention.

But Jesus said, "I have a greater witness than John's" (John 5:36), and here Jesus gave a trifecta of witnesses. First, His *works*, the ones He was doing on the Sabbath, testified that the Father had sent Him (John 5:36). The religious leaders certainly should've picked up on this, but they were so stuck on their own purity laws that they couldn't see what God was saying through the miracles of Jesus. Second, the Father Himself testified, saying, "This is my beloved Son, in whom I am well pleased" (Matt 3:17), but they were incapable of hearing what the Father was saying because they wouldn't hear His Son. Finally (and this is the one that really left no excuse for these teachers of the law), the Scriptures testified about Jesus, and they were the Scripture experts of their day, hoping to find life in its pages. Still, they refused to hear what the Scripture said about Jesus, the Giver of life.

Jesus concluded His address to these religious leaders by saying that He wasn't going to accuse them before the Father; He would leave that to Moses. "For if you believed Moses, you would believe Me; for he wrote about Me. But if you do not believe his writings, how will you believe My words?" (John 5:46-47). Ouch.

APPLICATION

Do you want to get well? Jesus asked this question to the disabled man by the pool of Bethesda, and he said yes. After 38 years, he was ready to be well. Sin is powerfully deceptive; we start down the path of evil because sin has convinced us that it is the way to life, but in the end it leads only to destruction (Prov 14:12).

Here's the question you want to wrestle with: "Are you still under sin's spell?" That is, "Do you want to be made well, or are you happy in your sin?" You may not need to dig too deeply to find a sin that they have been holding on to. Jesus *wants* to make us well, but we must want to be made well too.

ADDITIONAL NOTES

Some translations exclude John 5:4 from their text on account of the fact that it is not found in several of the oldest manuscripts. Verse 4, however, is included in a vast majority of manuscripts even if it is not in the small number of very early manuscripts that remain (many, many more were not preserved). Regardless, without this verse, the passage makes little sense (verse 7 seems to refer back to it).

ACTIVITIES

1. Testimonies of Jesus. We should not believe a person's claims about himself based only on his own testimony. He needs someone else to testify about him or have evidence to back up his claims. Read John 5:31-46 and answer the following questions.

Make a list of all the different evidences that Jesus says testify about Him in John 5:31-46. _____
_____
_____
_____
_____
_____
_____
_____
_____
_____
_____

Unit 3: Jesus' Popularity Grows

Make a list of some other testimonies about Jesus, not included in John 5:31-46.

_____
_____
_____
_____
_____
_____
_____
_____

Which evidence do you find most convincing and why?

_____
_____
_____
_____
_____
_____
_____
_____

Lesson 3.4

EVALUATION

1. Why doesn't John say what feast this was? _____
_____

2. What feast was it and what clues does John give to help get us there?_____
_____
_____
_____
_____

3. Why would sick and disabled people collect by this pool? _____
_____

4. Why had the man not been healed there after 38 years?_____

5. What did Jesus ask him before He healed him?_____

6. What did Jesus say to the man to heal him? _____

7. On what day did this miracle occur? _____

8. How did the religious leaders respond when they saw the man walking? _____
_____

9. What did the religious leaders say to Jesus when they found out He had healed the man?_____
_____

10. How did Jesus respond to their accusation? _____
_____

11. Why was Jesus pushing the religious leaders so hard?_____
_____

12. What did Jesus say about His relationship with the Father? _____
_____

13. What was the one testimony that the religious leaders really should have heard and received? ____
_____

LESSON 3.5

Jesus Chose and Taught His Disciples

UNIT 3

THE STORY

Lesson Theme - Jesus shifted from an independent ministry model to a focused discipleship training model because His disciples began to imitate Him.

In this lesson we see that although Jesus' Galilean ministry continued, there was a significant shift in Jesus' focus. In the early portion of His ministry, Jesus was basically acting independently. He was gathering a following of disciples as He went and specifically selecting a few as *close* followers, but they were there to watch and learn. In this portion of His ministry, some of His disciples began to agitate the Pharisees in the same way Jesus had been—breaking their sacred, but manmade purity rules. As a result, Jesus stepped up the discipleship training. He selected twelve of His disciples, designated them as apostles, and began training them to be sent out. He continued to do much of the same kind of ministry, but His selected twelve were in training rather than just following a good teacher around.

Jesus had gained a number of followers during His early Galilean ministry. Some of these had faithfully followed Him from town to town, seeing Him perform miracles and agitate the religious leaders. Many of Jesus' closest followers would have traveled to Jerusalem for the Feast of Tabernacles and would have seen Him intentionally agitate the teachers of the law by healing a man on the Sabbath. These followers were starting to understand and incorporate Jesus' message into their lives. The Law was meant to bring life, not bondage. The teachers of the law were not faithfully preserving God's truth;

OVERVIEW

Jesus had been agitating the religious leaders throughout His Galilean ministry and even more so when He went to Jerusalem. His disciples were starting to catch on, and they imitated Jesus by plucking grain on the Sabbath—therefore breaking one of the rules of the religious leaders. Jesus saw this as a good sign; His followers were starting to do what He did. So He chose twelve and called them apostles; these were the ones He was going to send out *to do the same kinds of things He had done—miracles and all*. After teaching His disciples, Jesus performed two of the greatest miracles that He had done to date—healing a man from a distance and raising a widow's son from the dead. Imagine what His apostles who were going to be sent out to do these kinds of things might have been thinking! Jesus was preparing His followers to do great things.

SOURCE MATERIAL

- Luke 6:1-7:17

they were missing the whole point and making the people of Israel into slaves. Many of the Sabbath laws the Israelites had been taught to obey in their religious training as children were just manmade purity rules.

Jesus' disciples went from simply listening to His teaching and watching His actions to imitating Him. They wanted to push the buttons of the religious leaders in the same way Jesus had. "Now

Unit 3: Jesus' Popularity Grows

OBJECTIVES

Feel...

- impressed that Jesus' disciples were imitating Him.
- grateful that Jesus chose disciples to be sent out.
- amazed at the greatness of Jesus' miracles.

Understand...

- that the disciples were not just hungry, they were intentionally breaking man made rules when they plucked grain on the Sabbath.
- what Jesus was claiming about Himself and His disciples when He drew a comparison to David and his companions.
- why Jesus might have thought that this was a good time to select apostles.
- why Jesus increased the potency of His miracles at this point.
- what the disciples would have been thinking as Jesus increased the potency of His miracles.

Apply this understanding by...

- learning to love as Jesus loves so you can someday confront as Jesus confronts.

it happened on the second Sabbath after the first that He went through the grainfields. And His disciples plucked the heads of grain and ate them" (Luke 6:1). The disciples knew that they were breaking several of the Pharisees' Sabbath regulations, and they knew it would provoke a response. Sure enough, the Pharisees challenged them, "Why are you doing what is not lawful to do on the Sabbath?" (Luke 6:2).

Jesus answered for His disciples, "Have you not even read this, what David did when he was hungry, he and those who were with him: how he went into the house of God, took and ate the showbread, and also gave some to those with him, which is not lawful for any but the priests to eat?" (Luke 6:3-4). Jesus could have defended His disciples by simply pointing out that the Pharisees' Sabbath regulations were made up rules; the disciples weren't really breaking the Sabbath. But much like He did with the religious leaders in Jerusalem when He healed the invalid at the sheep gate pool, He pushed it further; He wanted the Pharisees to have to wrestle with His identity.

In order to do this, Jesus drew a comparison between Himself and David. David had been anointed as king, but he hadn't taken the throne yet; God still had Saul on the throne. Saul was jealous of David and actively trying to kill him, so David had to flee. He fled with some of his closest followers and went to the tabernacle which at that time was set up at Nob. When he arrived, he asked the priest for some bread, claiming they were on a special mission from the king. There was no ordinary bread available, but the bread of the presence which had been set before the Lord was available. This bread was ordinarily reserved for the priests to eat since they were holy. David and his men were permitted to eat this bread even though it technically broke the rules because of *who David was*.

Likewise, Jesus said, "The Son of Man is also Lord of the Sabbath" (Luke 6:5). Jesus was making an incredibly bold claim here. He was not only saying that He was the new David, the anointed King, and His disciples were like David's mighty men of battle. He was also saying that He was Creator of the Sabbath and therefore the Pharisees' rules didn't apply to Him; He knew what the Sabbath was really all about. He clarified on another Sabbath what He was talking about by asking the Pharisees, "Is it lawful on the Sabbath to do good or to do evil, to save life or to destroy it?" (Luke 6:9). The Sabbath was always meant to be a life-giving feast, but their rules sucked the life out of it.

It was no accident that Jesus selected His twelve disciples after they had provoked the Pharisees by plucking grain on the Sabbath (Luke 6:12-16). His disciples had been watching Jesus long enough to start imitating Him; they had proven that they were ready for more intensive and personal teaching and training. Jesus wanted disciples who not only wanted to learn from Him; He wanted disciples He could send out. (That is what the word "apostle" means in Luke 6:13.)

So Jesus gathered His twelve around Him along with a large crowd of His disciples and proceeded to teach them. This discourse is called the Sermon on the Plain (Luke 6:13-49). A number of scholars believe that Jesus taught this sermon on exactly the same occasion as the Sermon on the Mount in Matthew. This interpretation makes some sense; the content is very similar. Furthermore, the nature of the geography in Galilee can account for it being called both the Sermon on the Mount and the Sermon on the Plain—it is possible that Jesus was standing on a wide flat place on a mountainside.

We interpret, however, that Jesus preached these sermons on two different occasions. The content of these sermons was Jesus' basic discipleship training material, and He probably preached something similar on a number of occasions. Here, Jesus preached this material to His disciples who had just proven that they were starting to "get" what Jesus' mission was all about; they were prepared to hear it with fresh ears. The reality is, these sermons are the kind of thing you need to hear a number of times before you really start to understand what Jesus was talking about. We are not going to dig into the content of the Sermon on the Plain since we covered this content when we looked at the Sermon on the Mount.

Jesus had now officially called His twelve closest followers; He had His mighty men like David did, and His ministry in Galilee continued. Like before, He continued to travel throughout Galilee, healing the sick, preaching the gospel and raising the dead. But everything looked different to His closest twelve whom He had called as apostles (sent-out ones). They were now seeing everything Jesus was doing and thinking about the possibility of doing those kind of things themselves. Imagine their excitement and fear as they watched Jesus perform miracles.

With this background, Jesus' next two miracles become much more interesting. Jesus knew that His closest twelve apostles were watching with a bit of trepidation, knowing that they would be sent out to perform miracles as well. Jesus had demonstrated a habit of anticipating the reactions of the Pharisees and teachers of the law and then doing things to amplify their reactions; He liked to push buttons. He did the same thing to His disciples here. Up to this point, Jesus would heal the sick people who came to Him and cast out demons of those brought to Him, but now He took it to the next level. A centurion came to Jesus asking Him to heal his servant, and Jesus didn't even go to his home. The centurion simply returned to the house to find his servant healed (Luke 7:1-10). Soon afterwards, Jesus approached a town called Nain and raised a widow's dead son (Luke 7:11-15). This was the first time Jesus had raised *anyone* from the dead,

Unit 3: Jesus' Popularity Grows

and the widow hadn't even asked Him to heal her son.

Jesus had performed many miracles by this point, but these two provoked a new level of interest throughout Israel. People were beginning to realize that Jesus wasn't just a miracle worker there to heal their diseases; He was a great prophet and some kind of a deliverer (Luke 1:16-17).

APPLICATION

Gentle Jesus, meek and mild. We often think of Him that way, but many of the stories in the gospels show Him agitating the sanctimonious, rebuking those in power, and being generally destructive of religious traditions and established cultural expectations. If your are going to be like Jesus, they will need to learn to do likewise. Jesus' disciples, though perhaps not as bold, started doing what Jesus did; they knew they were breaking sacred rules when they plucked and ate grain on the Sabbath. They were imitating Jesus.

Now, a couple of points to balance this out. Jesus didn't start pushing these boundaries until He was at least 30 years old; and then He was doing it when He had the respect of the crowds and some credibility with the religious leaders. This kind of thing takes maturity and a serious track record. Furthermore, Jesus *never* broke the actual commandments of God; He never did anything on the Sabbath that was forbidden by God, and the things He did were really the main point of the Sabbath law—giving rest to the weary. Finally, though He could be hard on these religious leaders, He loved them... He loved them deeply. He desperately wanted to have peace with them (Luke 13:34). These heart and obedience issues are absolute prerequisites to agitating the self-righteous.

Learning to love as Jesus loved and obey as Jesus obeyed is your starting place on the path toward rebuking as Jesus rebuked. If we aren't praying for the sanctimonious, then we can't confront them. And we will be judged with the standard with which we judge others. If you want to be as bold as Jesus someday, you must learn to be as loving as Jesus today.

ACTIVITIES

1. Journal Time. Spend some time thinking, praying and writing about the following in the space below:

Jesus could confront the Pharisees because He loved them first. He also waited until He had matured and earned the respect of the people. Think of a person or group of people that you wish you could confront like Jesus confronted the Pharisees. Now spend some time praying that God would give you the ability to love this person (or people) the way Jesus loved people. Write out your prayer for this person (or people). _____

_____

_____

_____

_____

_____

_____

2. Personal Reflection: Becoming the Superhero. The goal of this activity is to get you inside this story—to see yourself as the disciples and imagine what might have been going through their heads. In order to do this, we will use some popular superheroes. Imagine what it would take to become like these mythical heroes. In order to do this, we are going to work from self-made superheroes to the more supernatural kind. _____

Imagine you are an apprentice of Batman or Iron Man. What would it take to become a superhero like them? _____

_____

_____

Imagine you are an apprentice of Spider-Man. What would it take to become a superhero like him? ___

_____

_____

Unit 3: Jesus' Popularity Grows

Imagine you are an apprentice of Superman. What would it take to become a superhero like him? _____

Jesus is greater than all these superheroes. In this lesson, He healed a man from a distance and raised a widow's son from the dead—He has power over death. And yet, He called twelve of His closest followers *apostles*. This meant that they would be asked to do the same miracles He did. What would it take to become like Jesus, not just in character, but in power? _____

Lesson 3.5

EVALUATION

1. Did the disciples know that it would frustrate the religious leaders when they plucked grain on the Sabbath? _____
_____
_____

2. Then why did they do it? _____
_____
_____

3. When Jesus responded to the religious leaders, He compared Himself and His disciples to David and his companions. What was He trying to get across by this comparison? _____
_____
_____

4. Why do you think Jesus chose His twelve apostles right after this? _____
_____
_____

5. What is the main difference between the Sermon on the Plain in Luke and the Sermon on the Mount in Matthew? _____
_____
_____
_____

6. Why do you think Jesus might have followed His choosing of the apostles with such great miracles? _____
_____

7. What do you think the apostles might have been thinking when Jesus raised the dead? _____
_____
_____

UNIT 4: JESUS REJECTED

Jesus had become a well known character in Israel; everyone knew about Him. And His message had divided His audience—His closest disciples were firmly committed to Him, and many crowds were following Him; but the religious establishment had had enough. In a calculated move, they attributed Jesus' ability to cast a demon out of a deaf mute to the power of Beelzebub, the prince of demons. Jesus rebuked them for blaspheming the Holy Spirit and called them to repent, but they wouldn't. This represents the turning point in Jesus' ministry; the leaders of Israel had rejected the Messiah.

Having been rejected by the religious leaders, Jesus focused His attention more closely on His followers through whom He would now bring the kingdom. This focus entailed speaking in parables, which would hide the truth from those who rejected Him. The parables in Matthew 13 are descriptions of what was happening to the kingdom during Jesus' lifetime—Israel's leaders had rejected the kingdom, and so Jesus would bring the kingdom to earth through His followers as a "new people."

Jesus' focus was also on building His disciples' faith. Miracle after miracle demonstrated that Jesus had power over sickness, demons and even death. He then gave the twelve apostles authority over demons and sent them out to do what He had been doing. But this was more than just a "trial run"; Jesus gave them authority to accept or reject cities and individuals on behalf of the kingdom. Meanwhile, Jesus' reputation as a powerful and important man was being established at higher levels; something, they thought, was going to have to be done about Him.

As time progressed, Jesus was rejected, not just by the religious leaders, but also by the crowds of followers He had attracted. One particular miracle, the feeding of the 5,000, made Jesus very popular for the wrong reasons. In order to continue on His mission without being encumbered by an army of 5,000 men trying to make Him king, Jesus challenged their spiritual dullness. They found this offensive and rejected Him.

Jesus was left with a small group of close followers who still needed intense training if they were going to be agents of the kingdom after Jesus ascended. Over the course of His later ministry, Jesus taught them how to properly challenge the religious leaders, how to pray in faith and trust God for provision. And, perhaps most importantly, He taught them (1) the principle of baptism—that true life and even glory can only come through death; and (2) the path to true greatness passes through failure and requires childlike humility and faith. These are the truths that would be driven home to the disciples through Jesus' death and resurrection.

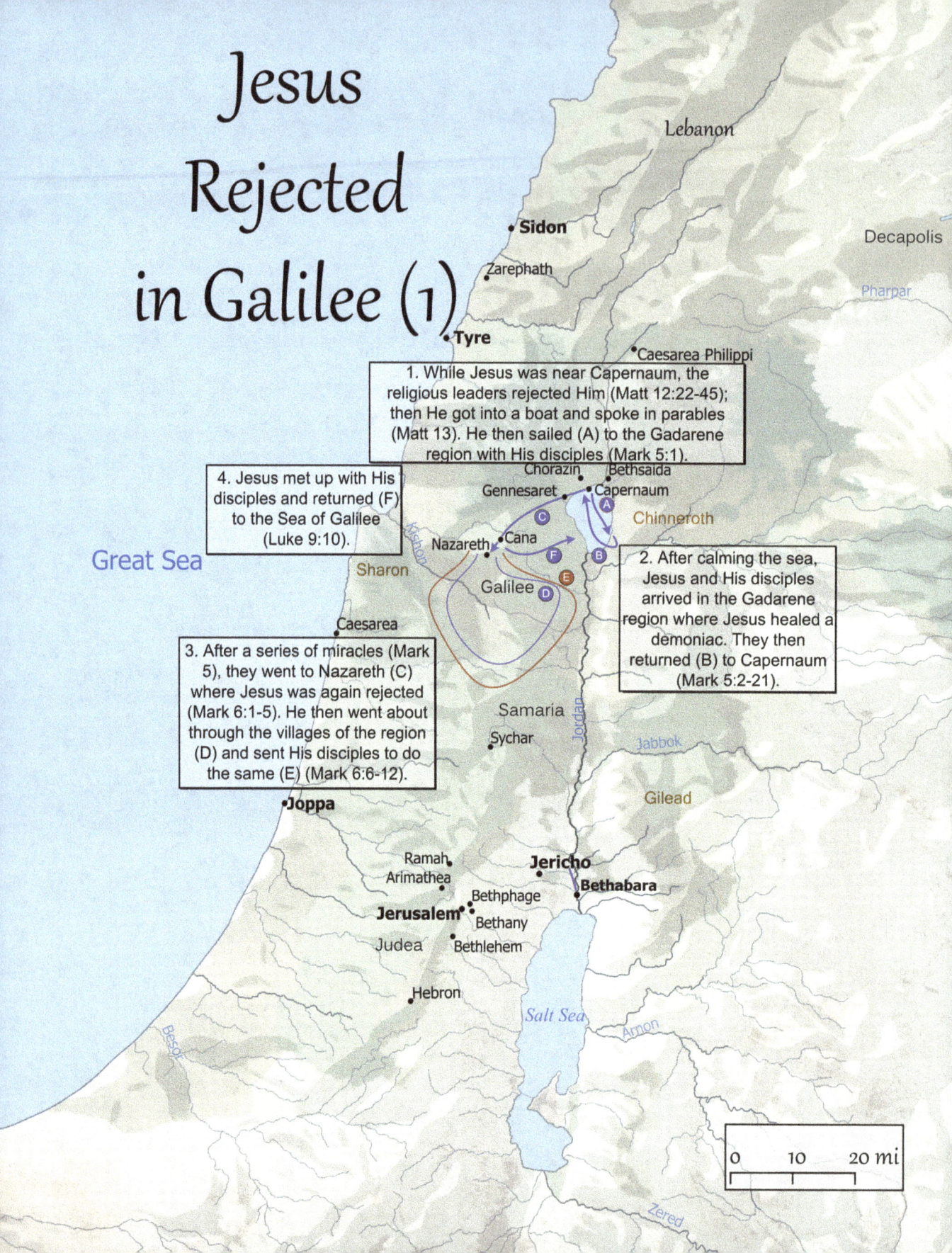

LESSON 4.1

The Turning Point: Galilee Rejected Jesus

UNIT 4

THE STORY

Lesson Theme - The religious leaders led the generation into denial of Christ.

The previous lesson ended with Jesus performing some of the most staggering miracles He had up to this point. People were amazed and many were beginning to believe that He was more than just a miracle worker; maybe He was the great prophet: the Messiah of God. This was good news, but every action brings an equal and opposite reaction. As more people believed in Jesus, more people were calcified into their stiff opposition to Him. This was especially true of the religious leaders whose opposition to Jesus only increased as His popular support increased. Everything Jesus did undermined their system of religious control; they felt it to be an absolute necessity to bring an end to Jesus' popular following.

Jesus' desire was that the religious leaders, not just the crowds, would turn to Him and repent of their sins. In fact, full repentance couldn't happen without the religious leaders repenting as well. They were the ones who ran the synagogues and oversaw worship at the temple. They were the ones God had entrusted with the position of spiritual leadership in Israel. Without their repentance, Israel, *as a nation*, could not repent.

In His early Galilean ministry, Jesus was going from town to town preaching in the synagogues. But this was no longer happening; Jesus was apparently not permitted to preach in many of the synagogues anymore. He had been rejected

OVERVIEW

Jesus' message had divided His audience; His closest disciples were firmly committed to Him, and many crowds were following Him; but the religious establishment was ready to reject Him. The religious leaders were capable of casting out demons, but believed that only the Messiah could cast out a mute demon. When Jesus accomplished this feat, they attributed His ability to Beelzebub, the prince of demons. Jesus rebuked them for blaspheming the Holy Spirit and called them to repent. This represented a turning point in Jesus' ministry; the nation, that generation of Israel, had rejected the Messiah. Jesus in turn rejected them and moved to build a new people out of His followers.

SOURCE MATERIAL

- **Matthew 12:22-12:45**
- Mark 3:22-35
- Jonah 3
- Psalm 32

in town after town by their religious leaders. To be sure, He maintained a strong following among the crowds, but on an official level, He had been rejected.

The Messianic miracle
As both His support and His opposition were reaching record levels, a demon-possessed man who was both blind and mute was brought to

Unit 4: Jesus Rejected

OBJECTIVES

Feel...

- awe at Jesus' power.
- sadness that the religious leaders rejected Jesus.
- joy that Jesus moved to build a new people out of His followers.

Understand...

- why it was important for Jesus to be accepted by the religious leaders.
- that Jesus confirmed His identity as Messiah in terms the religious leaders would understand—by healing a mute demoniac.
- what the blasphemy of the Holy Spirit is (in general) and what exactly the religious leaders did to commit it in this story.
- why blasphemy against the Holy Spirit is a bigger deal than blasphemy against the Son of Man.
- that Jesus was calling the religious leaders to repentance for committing blasphemy against the Holy Spirit.
- that at a corporate level, the religious leaders' rejection of Jesus represented a generational rejection of Him.
- that Jesus turned His attention to His followers as the beginning of a "new people" following this corporate rejection.
- the importance of repentance on both a corporate and individual level.

Apply this understanding by...

- becoming "quick to repent."
- repenting of any sin the Lord brings to your attention.

Jesus to be healed (Matt 12:22). Exorcisms were not all that uncommon in that day. Obviously, Jesus had cast out many demons, but even the Pharisees and teachers of the law had the ability to cast out demons. Their method of casting out was a three step process. First, they would establish communication with the demon. Second, they would ask the demon's name. Once they knew the name of the demon, they could address it by name to cast it out.

If a demon caused a person to be unable to speak, the religious leaders couldn't cast that demon out. If there was no way to establish communication, they couldn't order the demon to leave. The rabbis taught that when the Messiah came, He would be able to cast out this type of demon.

It was exactly this type of demon-possessed person who was brought to Jesus on this occasion. If Jesus could cast this demon out and heal the man, He would have validated the fact that He was the Messiah on the terms of the religious leaders. It was *their* literature that said that the Messiah would be able to cast a mute demon out of a person. With tensions as high as they were and a test of this magnitude before Jesus, the stakes were *really* high. If Jesus cast this demon out, He would have proven that He was the Messiah, and the religious leaders would be forced to admit that He was indeed the Messiah.

Blasphemy against the Holy Spirit
So Jesus cast out the demon, and what response did He get? The crowds said, "Could this be the Son of David?" (Matt 12:23). But the Pharisees said, "This fellow does not cast out demons except by Beelzebub, the ruler of the demons" (Matt 12:24). Unbelievable! Think about what the Pharisees had just done—they had invented a master explanation for Jesus' works. What mir-

Unit 4: Jesus Rejected

acle could Jesus now perform that they couldn't explain away with this simple piece of reasoning: "He did it by the power of Satan"?

But what had they *really* done? What had this explanation cost them? They had just attributed works that Jesus did by the power of the Holy Spirit to Satan. Instead of bowing down to Jesus whose identity had just been validated by the Spirit, they said, "He has an unclean spirit" (Mark 3:30). In short, they had blasphemed, or spoken against, the Holy Spirit. This was a *big* problem.

Jesus called them to Himself and immediately began to reason with them (Mark 3:23). It's important to see what Jesus was doing here; He was trying to reason with these Pharisees so that they would see the mistake they were making and repent. They had committed blasphemy against the Holy Spirit, and Jesus was calling them to turn from their sin. It was important that He do this quickly. Since blasphemy against the Holy Spirit is a master explanation, even providing a "reasonable" explanation for incredible miracles, it is not easy to escape from. Once someone is on the inside of that belief system it is hard to get out, and the longer they are there, the more difficult it becomes. So Jesus tried to talk them out of it. "If Satan casts out Satan, he is divided against himself. How then will his kingdom stand? And if I cast out demons by Beelzebub, by whom do your sons cast them out?" (Matt 12:26-27). The religious leaders' master explanation was not such a sensible explanation after all. It didn't make sense that Satan would drive out demons, and if Jesus was casting out demons by the power of Satan, wasn't the same true of the Pharisees' own exorcists? That sword cut both ways.

At this point, Jesus took the rhetoric up a notch. "Therefore I say to you, every sin and blasphemy will be forgiven men, but the blasphemy against the Spirit will not be forgiven men. Anyone who speaks a word against the Son of Man, it will be forgiven him; but whoever speaks against the Holy Spirit, it will not be forgiven him, either in this age or in the age to come" (Matt 12:31-32).

These verses have been the source of much concern. They have raised both theological questions: "How can a sin be so bad that Jesus' blood doesn't cover it?" and practical questions: "What if I committed this sin when I....?" The key to understanding this passage is to remember what Jesus was doing here: He was calling the Pharisees to repentance. They *had* committed blasphemy against the Holy Spirit, and Jesus was calling them to repentance so that they could be forgiven. Nowhere in this passage does it say that this sin is unforgivable. Of course it can be forgiven; that's why Jesus died! But the Pharisees *would not be forgiven* if they didn't repent.

Jonah did something similar when he preached at Nineveh, "Yet forty days, and Nineveh shall be overthrown!" he announced (Jonah 3:4). He did not add, "unless you repent." He didn't need to; the announcement of judgement *was* a call to repentance. The people repented, and Nineveh was saved.

The same thing is going on in Matthew 12. Jesus was calling the Pharisees to repentance in the strongest possible terms because He loved them and wanted them to repent.

One final question to address is: why would Jesus say that blasphemy against the Son of Man would be forgiven while blasphemy against the Holy Spirit would not? If Jesus, the Son of God, came along making claims about Himself, saying, "I am the Messiah," without backing it up with any miracles, His critics couldn't be blamed for saying, "That guy is a nut." It would be blasphemy against the Son of Man, but it would be understandable. As Jesus said elsewhere, "If I bear witness of Myself, My witness is not true" (John 5:31). People claiming to be the Messiah were a dime a dozen in Jesus' day; miracles (signs) were *the* way to validate Messianic claims, because they demonstrated that the Holy Spirit was at work in the one making the claims. When a person denies the Spirit, he has cut himself off from being convinced; he has cut himself off from *God*. Repentance is possible, but the deeper one goes into blasphemy against the Spirit, the more difficult it is to get out.

A generational sin
In response to Jesus' call to repentance, the Pharisees and teachers of the law asked Jesus for a sign. This was an odd request; Jesus had performed many signs and had just cast a mute demon out of a man. He could perform another sign, but it is not hard to anticipate their response: "See, we told you He has the power of Beelzebub!" In response, Jesus said, "An evil and adulterous generation seeks after a sign" (Matt 12:39). Jesus was *not* saying, "If any generation asks for a sign, that is an evil and adulterous generation." Seeking signs is a good thing if your heart is pure; that is the only way Jesus could have validated His claims to those who were seeking the Messiah. His was a statement of shock and disbelief; He was saying, "What!!? An evil generation wants a sign??! Ridiculous!"

Notice that in Matthew 12:39-42, Jesus moved from addressing their rejection of Him as an individual sin to addressing their rejection as a generational sin. The Pharisees and teachers of the law were putting Jesus on notice, telling Him He had been rejected as their Messiah. He had many followers among the common people, but the religious leaders had rejected Him... the nation had rejected Him.

In response, Jesus put *them* on notice, telling them that this generation was under judgement. Nineveh repented at Jonah's preaching, but this generation wouldn't repent when someone greater than Jonah preached to them. Even Nineveh was in a position to judge this wicked generation. Jesus came to clean this generation of their demons, but since they wouldn't accept Jesus, the demons would only return in greater number than before.

This represents a significant shift in Jesus' ministry. He came as the new Israel to reach the old Israel; He was there to speak to His family. But His family had rejected Him. So, His attention now turned to a new family, a new Israel. His followers were His new family, and they were the seed that would grow into a new kingdom.

As Jesus was still addressing the Pharisees, someone informed Him that His family was waiting outside to speak to Him. His response was in the form of a parable; it symbolized Him turning from Israel as a nation to His followers as a new people. "'Who is My mother and who are My brothers?' And He stretched out His hand toward His disciples and said, 'Here are My mother and My brothers! For whoever does the will of My Father in heaven is My brother and sister and mother'" (Matt 12:48-50).

APPLICATION

This lesson, in many ways, is about the importance of repentance. The religious leaders who were there when Jesus healed the mute demoniac had a clear call to repentance from Jesus, and they refused. The consequences of that action were quick and serious, but ripple on down through the ages to this day. A remnant was chosen in place of the nation.

The same is true of repentance in the lives of individual Christians. The longer we live in sin and refuse opportunities to repent, the harder it is to get out of the sin, and the deeper the consequences get.

ADDITIONAL NOTES: DEALING WITH "UNFORGIVABLE SIN" FEARS

Many Christians have gone through a period in their lives where, based on this passage, they were afraid they had committed the "unforgivable sin." The first and most important answer to this question comes by just looking closely at the text. There is nothing in here that says the sin was "unforgivable." It does say that someone who commits blasphemy against the Holy Spirit "will not be forgiven" (Matt 12:32), and this is absolutely true *if they don't repent*. But even unbelievers will be forgiven of this sin if they repent; *that is what Jesus was calling the religious leaders to do*. The same is true for believers; if a believer commits blasphemy against the Holy Spirit, he should *simply repent*.

There are many theories on exactly what the "unforgivable sin" is; some say it's suicide, some say it's divorce, some say murder... the list goes on and on. Forget all that; this passage tells us exactly what the sin is that God won't forgive unless you repent (again, it doesn't say it is unforgivable)—it is blasphemy against the Holy Spirit, which is simply speaking against the Holy Spirit. The religious leaders were guilty of a particularly egregious form of this sin; but many people, *even Christians,* have committed lesser versions of it. Many Christians have repented and been forgiven of this sin as well.

What happens if a Christian commits this sin and never repents? Well, first of all, don't be that Christian. The clue in this passage comes in Matthew 12:36: "But I tell you that *everyone* will have to give an account for every empty word they have spoken" (NIV, emphasis added). Both Christians and unbelievers alike will be judged—Christians at the judgement seat of Christ (2 Cor 5:10) and unbelievers at the great white throne. As 2 Corinthians 5:10 says, every believer will receive judgement for what he has done while in the body. Some will be rewarded greatly, some little, and some will be rebuked. Those who have committed blasphemy against the Holy Spirit will be judged at this time too. All believers will enter life, but not all will be rewarded.

ACTIVITIES

1. Compare and Contrast: Ninevites and Pharisees. Read Jonah 3 and Matthew 12:31-32. Then make a list of as many similarities and differences between the Ninevites and Pharisees as you can.

Ninevites	Pharisees

Unit 4: Jesus Rejected

2. Repentance Psalm. Sing or read Psalm 32 which is one of David's psalms of repentance. Spend some time praying and reflecting on this psalm; then write your prayers and repentance in the space below._____

_____

_____

_____

_____

_____

3. Theological Reflection. This passage is commonly used to teach that there is some sin, or sins, that God *cannot* forgive—called the "unforgivable sin." We have made the case that this passage teaches no such thing (it never says that the sin is unforgivable, and Jesus was calling those who committed blasphemy against the Holy Spirit to repentance). For some, the question will still remain—does Jesus really forgive *every* sin? Let's dig in.

What is the worst possible sin that you can imagine?_____

_____

According to Romans 5:20 is there any sin which could possibly outrun God's grace?_____

_____

_____

_____

Do you believe that Jesus died even for the worst possible sin?_____

_____

_____

_____

Do you think the worst possible sin is forgivable based on Romans 5:20?_____

_____

_____

_____

Lesson 4.1

EVALUATION

1. Why did Jesus seek to prove to the religious leaders that He was the Messiah? _____

2. What point was Jesus making when He healed a mute demoniac? _____

3. What is blasphemy against the Holy Spirit? _____

4. Why is blasphemy against the Holy Spirit a bigger deal than blasphemy against the Son of Man? _____

5. Why did Jesus call the religious leaders to Himself to reason with them; what was He hoping to get out of the conversation? _____

    What was He calling them to repentance for? _____

6. The individuals who committed blasphemy against the Holy Spirit were called to repentance; beyond that, what did their rejection of Jesus mean for the nation? _____

7. How did Jesus respond to the national rejection of Him? To whom did He turn? _____

LESSON 4.2

The Parables of the Kingdom

UNIT 4

THE STORY

Lesson Theme - Israel's history and the parables
Jesus had been rejected by the leadership of Israel and now turned His attention to creating a new people from His followers. From this point on, Jesus spoke regularly in parables.

Parables are often thought to be quaint illustrations that connect to the common man by simple analogy. In reality however, Jesus' parables are not the simplest teachings of Jesus; they are actually the most difficult to understand. When His disciples asked Him why He was speaking in parables, here is what Jesus told them:

> Because the knowledge of the secrets of the kingdom of heaven has been given to you, but not to them. Whoever has will be given more, and they will have an abundance. Whoever does not have, even what they have will be taken from them. This is why I speak to them in parables: "Though seeing, they do not see; though hearing, they do not hear or understand." (Matt 13:11-13, NIV)

The string of parables in Matthew 13 are kingdom parables. Almost all of them begin with "The kingdom of heaven is like..." and then continue with an analogy of some aspect of the kingdom. Before we dig too deeply into these parables, we need to figure out what Jesus meant by "kingdom of heaven."

OVERVIEW

Having been rejected by the religious leaders, Jesus turned His attention to His followers through whom He would now bring the kingdom. Jesus began speaking in parables so that His followers would understand what He was saying, but the truth would be hidden from those who rejected Him. The parables in Matthew 13 are descriptions of what was happening to the kingdom during Jesus' lifetime more than they are principles of how the kingdom would operate in the apostolic age. Israel, as a nation, had rejected the kingdom, and so Jesus planned to bring the kingdom to earth through His followers as a "new people."

SOURCE MATERIAL

- Matthew 12:46-13:52

Kingdom of heaven
Since the beginning of Genesis, God has been in the kingdom business. God made man and told him to rule over the earth. Adam messed it up, and mankind ended up with a kingdom built without reference to God—the whole earth in the years before Noah and the kingdom of Babel afterwards. Whatever *kingdom of heaven* means, it certainly isn't these manmade kingdoms without reference to God.

Jesus told us to pray, "Thy kingdom come, Thy will be done, on earth as it is in heaven," but long before He gave us those words, God had been working toward that goal. Notice that these

Unit 4: Jesus Rejected

OBJECTIVES

Feel...

- excited that Jesus was building His kingdom around His followers.
- thankful for the way the kingdom works.

Understand...

- that the parables are about Israel's history, and Jesus was the culmination of the story.
- that parables are not quaint stories to illustrate truth, but a way to hide truth from those who have rejected Jesus.
- how to interpret parables.
- what the parables mean.

Apply this understanding by...

- looking at your own life through the parable of the sower and determining what kinds of temptations are most likely to distract you from following Jesus.

---

parables are about the kingdom *of* heaven, not the kingdom *in* heaven. The focus is heavenly rule on earth.

The first step we get in the Bible toward a heavenly kingdom on earth is the call of Abram. God started by choosing one man and building a nation out of him. The kingdom of heaven on earth had started with the nation of Israel, but had now come to a turning point. Israel had rejected the Messiah. Of course, God was not going to cast off Israel forever (Rom 11:1-2), but, *as a nation*, Israel had rejected their Messiah. Jesus turned to a new aspect of the kingdom of heaven; He was going to build a new people out of His followers.

Matthew explains that by speaking in parables, Jesus was fulfilling an Old Testament prophecy, "I will open my mouth in parables, I will utter things hidden since the creation of the world" (Ps 78:2). In its context, this prophecy is saying that the psalmist was going to reveal what God had been doing throughout the history of Israel. Likewise, Jesus was speaking in parables, explaining what God had been doing in Israel's history and what He was doing in the current events in Israel. Jesus was helping His disciples understand how to navigate the transition from Israel, the nation, as the kingdom of heaven, to His followers as a new kingdom of heaven.

Interpreting the parables

In order to interpret the parables, you have to understand what Jesus was trying to do with them. Several principles are involved here.

First, Jesus used the parables to explain how the history of Israel had led to Israel's rejection of Him and therefore led Him to create a new people out of His followers. Therefore, you will often see that (1) Jesus is the main character in many of the parables, and (2) He comes at the end of the parables since He is taking place at the end of the story He is telling.

Second, many of the parables begin with "The kingdom of heaven is like," but that doesn't always mean that whatever comes after the "like" is a picture of the kingdom *as a whole*; it may just be a picture of an aspect of the kingdom.

Third, the parables are interdependent. It is often the case that one parable will help you figure out what another parable means. Furthermore, if an element is repeated in multiple parables, it will often have a similar meaning in each (e.g., seed).

The parables
The parable of the sower. Jesus is the farmer, and Israel is the field in which He scatters His seeds. The seeds are the gospel of the kingdom, and the four types of soil represent four ways people tend to respond to His preaching. The path represents the Pharisees, teachers of the law, and those who were opposed to Jesus from the beginning. They heard the gospel, but the evil one snached it away. The rocky soil represents the large crowds of followers Jesus gained early on. Here, the seeds of the gospel sprang up quickly but began to die out in them when they realized that following Jesus was going to be hard. The thorny soil represents those followers who were eager early on, but realized that they would have to give up wealth and happiness to follow Jesus. Finally, the good soil represents Jesus' disciples and other close followers. They were the few, the faithful, who would become the first of a new people. They would live lives that imitated Jesus and produced a huge harvest.

The parable of the wheat and the tares. The field, again, is Israel, and the man who sowed good seed in it is Jesus (Matt 13:37). The good seed are His faithful followers. The weeds are the Pharisees and teachers of the law; they are people who follow the evil one, and they are planted by the devil. In the time before the coming harvest, Jesus taught His disciples, "The harvest is plentiful but the workers are few. Ask the Lord of the harvest, therefore, to send out workers into His harvest field" (Matt 9:37-38). Jesus sent out His twelve disciples and then later the seventy, to separate between the wheat and the tares.

The parables of the mustard seed and the leaven. Here two parables have basically the same message. Jesus is the man who planted the mustard seed, and the mustard seed represents His disciples. He will "plant" His disciples, and the kingdom of heaven will grow from their work. Likewise, the leaven represents the disciples who will spread throughout the world to create the kingdom of heaven.

The parables of the hidden treasure and the pearl. In the first of these parables, Jesus is the man who bought the field. The field, again, is Israel, and the treasure represents His faithful followers who are the new people and a new kingdom. Jesus sold everything He had, even His life, to buy Israel so He could gain His followers. In the second, Jesus is the merchant, and the pearl of great price represents His disciples.

The parable of the net. This last parable is like the parable of the wheat and tares. The fish are the people of Israel. The "angels" (Greek: messengers) are Jesus' disciples sent throughout the land. The good fish are those who heard the message of the kingdom with faith, and the bad fish are those who rejected Jesus.

Notice Jesus' final statement, "Therefore every teacher of the law who has become a disciple of the kingdom of heaven is like the owner of a house who brings out of his storeroom new treasures as well as old" (Matt 13:52). The teachers of the law were those who were the keepers of the religious heritage of Israel. Most of these religious leaders were the seed that fell on the path, the tares and the bad fish of Jesus' parables. But those who turned to Jesus and became disciples of the kingdom would get all of the treasures of the kingdom without losing their treasures of the Law.

Unit 4: Jesus Rejected

APPLICATION

These parables are primarily about the state of Israel during Jesus' ministry, but they have broad application to our lives as individuals and the times we live in. Use the parable of the sower as a primary point of application for this lesson. Focus in on the rocky soil and the weedy soil. Determine what temptations are likely to try to try to pull you off the path of the righteous. See the activities for this application.

ACTIVITIES

1. Study the Soils. Jesus described four types of soils in His first parable (Matt 13:3-9, 18-23). The first (the path) represents soil that never sprouted life: unbelievers. The last (the fruitful soil) is what we are all aiming for. The two in the middle—the rocky soil and the thorny soil—teach us a lot about the temptations we will face in life that could pull us off the path of the righteous. Answer the following questions regarding the rocky and thorny soils.

What temptations does the rocky soil warn us about? _____
_____
_____

What does the plant in rocky soil need in order to prevent being uprooted when these trials come? __
_____
_____

What would "deeper roots" look like in your life? _____
_____
_____

What temptations does the soil that produces thorns warn you about? _____
_____
_____

What are some examples of "thorns" or worldly temptations that you might face in your life?_____
_____
_____

Lesson 4.2

What can you do to prepare for these temptations, so that they will not deceive you? _____
_____
_____
_____
_____

2. Journal Time. In the space below, write down a temptation/trial that you are struggling with or think you might struggle with in the future. Write down what you can do to protect yourself from that temptation. _____
_____
_____
_____
_____
_____
_____
_____
_____
_____

3. Interpret the Parables. Choose a parable from Matthew 13. Figure out what this parable means and answer the questions below.

Parable Title: _____

1. What does each major character or object in the parable represent? _____
_____
_____
_____
_____
_____
_____

Unit 4: Jesus Rejected

2. What is the meaning of the parable?

Lesson 4.2

EVALUATION

1. What are parables? _____
_____
_____

2. In general, what are the kingdom parables about? _____
_____
_____
_____

3. Describe two truths that help in interpreting the parables. _____
_____
_____
_____

4. Explain the meaning of one of the parables. _____
_____
_____
_____

LESSON 4.3

Jesus Built His Disciples' Faith

UNIT 4

THE STORY

Lesson Theme - Jesus produced fear and faith in His followers and in those who saw His miracles. This lesson is all about fear and faith. Now that the nation of Israel had rejected Him, Jesus worked to develop faith in His closest followers. Jesus' kingdom, which would now come into the world through His closest followers, was a kingdom of faith. Israel was a kingdom built on physical descendancy; Jesus' new kingdom was built on the faith of His followers. Faith is like one of those dimmer switches that clicks on, but the brightness can incrementally increase. The disciples had been switched on, but their faith was dim. Jesus was aiming to turn up the brightness. This lesson is about fear, because the path to faith in Jesus goes through fear of Him. In this lesson, we see that people were frightened at each of the miracles Jesus performed.

You want to step into the disciples' shoes and really try to see these miracles through their eyes, each miracle building on the ones before. Jesus had performed a lot of miracles in His ministry already... but this series of miracles is more intense. Not knowing Jesus better, one might think that He had lost control of His powers and was haphazardly healing anyone He came across. Jesus was literally radiating power at this point in His ministry.

Jesus had just finished an intense confrontation with the religious leaders followed immediately with an extended discourse of parables. He had been rejected and was now exhausted. He got into a boat to cross the Sea of Galilee with His

OVERVIEW

Having been rejected by the religious leaders, Jesus began to focus on building His disciples' faith. Jesus displayed the greatness of His power by calming a storm—demonstrating that He had power over creation, and by casting a "legion" of demons out of a man—demonstrating that He had power over the entire demonic realm. Following these miracles, a synagogue leader named Jairus asked Jesus to come heal his daughter. Along the way, Jesus was distracted when He *felt* power go out from Him to heal someone in the crowd. After He found out who caused this, Jesus commended her for her faith and continued on His way. By the time He arrived to heal Jairus' daughter, she was already dead. Jesus invited His three closest disciples into the room and raised her from the dead. Soon afterward, He arrived at His hometown, but was unable to perform very many miracles there because of their lack of faith.

SOURCE MATERIAL

Mark 4:35-6:6

disciples and immediately fell asleep. Meanwhile, a storm blew in. Several of His disciples were fishermen and had seen many storms on the Sea of Galilee, so the fact that they were afraid for their lives indicates how serious this storm was. Fishing boats on the Sea of Galilee in the first century were quite small, so it is surpris-

Unit 4: Jesus Rejected

OBJECTIVES

Feel...

- a sense of awe, even fear, at Jesus' staggering power.
- joy that Jesus was showing His great power to build His disciples' faith.

Understand...

- that Jesus was aiming to increase the strength of His disciples' faith.
- that the storm on the Sea of Galilee was really dangerous.
- that faith in Jesus is connected with fear of Him.
- that Jesus' power to calm the storm means that He is Lord of creation.
- that when Jesus healed the demoniac, He demonstrated power over demons.
- that when Jesus raised Jairus' daughter from the dead, He demonstrated that He had power over death.
- how the disciples might have felt as they saw Jesus perform these miracles in sequence.
- the relationship between faith and Jesus' ability to perform miracles.

Apply this understanding by...

- putting your faith in Jesus to do amazing things in your own life.

ing that Jesus would be sleeping through such a serious storm.

When the disciples finally woke Him up, Jesus simply rebuked the wind and the waves and said, "Peace, be still!" (Mark 4:39), and then rebuked the disciples for their fear and lack of faith. Their fear was misplaced; they shouldn't have been afraid of the storm, they should've been afraid of Jesus. And, as a result of this miracle, "they feared exceedingly" (Mark 4:41).

Jesus had performed many miracles by this point, but this miracle was somehow different to His disciples. He didn't pray and ask God to calm the storm; He spoke directly to the wind and the waves. He rebuked them, and they listened and obeyed. Jesus spoke and creation obeyed because He is the Lord of creation; the disciples began to understand this, saying, "Who can this be, that even the wind and the sea obey Him!" (Mark 4:41).

When they arrived at the region of the Gerasenes, a demoniac approached Jesus from the tombs. The people of the region had been unable to bind this man, so they just wrote him off and left him in the tombs. When he saw Jesus, he ran up and essentially bowed down before Him. As it turned out, this man didn't just have one demon, he had thousands. Symbolically here, the entire demonic realm was bowing down before Jesus and calling Him "Son of the Most High God" (Mark 5:7). Jesus had just shown that creation was under His power, and now He demonstrated that the demonic realm was under His authority. Jesus had cast out demons before, but those miracles just showed that Jesus had power over this demon or that; this miracle showed that Jesus had power over all demons. Jesus sent the demons into a herd of about 2,000 pigs that ran off a cliff into the lake.

The response from the locals was interesting. After those who were tending to the pigs ran off to tell them, the people came and pleaded with Jesus to leave the region. They were afraid; they "got it," but didn't like it. Perhaps they believed that Jesus was someone of divine power and importance, but didn't want to have to make room for someone so powerful in their lives. They believed, but they didn't believe. Nevertheless, Jesus would make His mark on the region—the man out of whom He had just cast the demons became a missionary to the region (Mark 5:19-20).

Jesus and the disciples then crossed the sea again where a synagogue leader named Jairus accosted Jesus to come heal his daughter who was near death. This man was clearly in a hurry to have Jesus heal his daughter so that she wouldn't die, and Jesus obliged and made His way with Jairus toward his house.

On the way, Jesus suddenly stopped and asked, "Who touched me?" (Mark 5:31). This seemed like an odd question to His disciples since He was surrounded on all sides by people who were touching Him. As it turned out, there was a woman there who had been bleeding for 12 years. She touched Jesus in faith and was healed; she had tapped into the power that Jesus was radiating. He stopped, commended her for her faith and continued on. The lesson is that Jesus' power is available to those who believe.

As Jesus and the woman were still speaking, it was reported to Jairus that he need not bother Jesus anymore because his daughter was dead. Jesus told Jairus, "Do not be afraid; only believe" (Mark 5:36). Jesus went into Jairus' house with Peter, James and John as well as the girl's parents and raised the girl from the dead. But He told them not to tell anyone; this miracle wasn't for everyone, only for those who had faith.

In contrast to these striking miracles and the faith that accompanied them, Jesus arrived at His hometown of Nazareth where His own people didn't believe in Him; they took offense at Him (see a similar event that occurred in Nazareth-Lesson 3.1). As a result of their unbelief, Jesus couldn't do very many miracles there and only healed a few people. Jesus had been almost unable to control His power in the previous stories; but now, because of the unbelief of the people in His hometown, He could hardly do anything. Lack of faith shut Jesus down.

Returning to the official rejection of Jesus in the previous lessons, the people of His hometown were like the people of Israel, and the people who believed in the previous miracles represented the "new people" He was creating out of His followers. The kingdom Jesus was bringing to earth operated on faith.

APPLICATION

Faith in Jesus isn't like an on/off switch; it's more like a dimmer switch. You have some amount of faith and (generally) you experience Christ in your life to the extent that you believe in Him. Your goal in this lesson is to "brighten" your faith, perhaps just a little, but increase it nonetheless. Use the faith stretcher activity below to help with this application.

Unit 4: Jesus Rejected

ACTIVITIES

1. Implications of Jesus' Miracles. Jesus used miracles to teach truths about Himself. Answer the following questions, using Mark 4:35-5:43 as a reference.

What does the fact that Jesus calmed the storm tell us about Jesus? _____
_____
_____

Jesus didn't pray and ask God to calm the storm, He directly commanded the storm to be still. What is the difference between simply praying for a miracle and commanding a miracle to happen? _____
_____
_____

When Jesus arrived on the other side of the sea, a man with thousands of demons came and fell on his knees before Him and made requests of Jesus. What does this tell us about Jesus? _____
_____
_____

In the story of Jairus' daughter, Jesus didn't pray that God would heal her, He simply commanded her to stand up. What does this tell us about Jesus? _____
_____
_____

2. Faith Stretcher. In the space below, write of a time when God did something miraculous in your life or in the life of someone you know. _____
_____
_____
_____
_____
_____
_____

Lesson 4.3

EVALUATION

1. Now that Israel had rejected Him, Jesus focused on training His disciples. In this lesson, what was the specific aim Jesus had for His disciples' growth? _____
_____
_____

2. Why is it important to "fear" Jesus as a part of increasing your faith in Him? _____
_____
_____

3. What does the fact that Jesus calmed the storm with a simple command tell us about who Jesus is?
_____
_____

4. What does Jesus' interaction with the demon-possessed man tell us about Jesus' relationship to the demonic forces? _____
_____
_____

5. What does Jesus' raising of Jairus' daughter tell us about Him? _____
_____
_____

6. How might the disciples have felt seeing this aggressive sequence of miracles? _____
_____
_____

7. What is the connection between the faith of the people and Jesus' ability to perform miracles?____
_____
_____
_____

LESSON 4.4

UNIT 4

Jesus Sent Out the Twelve Apostles

THE STORY

Lesson Theme - The outworking of the national rejection of Jesus and His commitment to building the kingdom through His followers

In many ways, Jesus' disciples had been in training since they first saw Him and started following Him, but there had been several instances where Jesus increased the stakes in their training. First, after the disciples imitated Him by plucking grain on the Sabbath, Jesus set apart twelve as apostles. In naming them apostles, Jesus was pointing toward the day when He would send them out—the word apostle means "one sent out." Immediately after the plucking of the grain, Jesus increased the power of the miracles He was performing, challenging the apostles to think about what they would be called to do. As a nation, Israel had rejected Jesus as their Messiah, and Jesus began to build His kingdom with these twelve apostles at the foundation. In this lesson, Jesus sends out the apostles, making good on naming them apostles.

Jesus continued to travel from village to village in Galilee, teaching and healing, but there was now an added layer to His ministry. Jesus called the twelve to Himself to send them out two-by-two (Mark 6:7). Their task was to divide between those who were a part of the kingdom and those who were destined for destruction. As He sent the pairs out, Jesus gave them authority over impure spirits—they were to cast out demons as they went.

OVERVIEW

Jesus gave the twelve apostles authority over demons and sent them out to do what He had been doing. But this was more than just a "trial run"; Jesus gave them authority to accept or reject cities and individuals on behalf of the kingdom. In short, if the city accepted them, the city was accepted; and if the city rejected them, they were to dust off their feet and depart from the city as though Jesus Himself had rejected it. Meanwhile, Jesus' reputation as a powerful and important man was being established at higher levels. In this lesson, we learn how Herod heard about Jesus and understood that something important was going on with Him.

SOURCE MATERIAL

- **Mark 6:6-31**
- Matthew 10:1-42

Jesus gave the twelve very specific instructions. Mark and Matthew both include different aspects of the instructions; the following list is a composite list of what Jesus told them:

1. Don't go to Gentiles or Samaritans, only to the lost sheep of Israel (Matt 10:5-6).
2. Preach the message: "The kingdom of heaven is at hand" (Matt 10:7).
3. Heal the sick, raise the dead, cleanse lepers and drive out demons (Matt 10:8).

Unit 4: Jesus Rejected

OBJECTIVES

Feel...

- excitement that Jesus was sending out the twelve apostles with power.
- amazed at the power that was given to the apostles both in terms of blessing and judgment.

Understand...

- that Jesus had been preparing the disciples to be sent out since the plucking of the grain on the Sabbath.
- that apostle means "one sent out."
- that the twelve were sent out to fulfill the parables of the wheat and tares: to make distinctions between followers of the kingdom and those who rejected Jesus.
- the instructions that Jesus gave to the disciples as they went out.
- that the sending out of the twelve disciples generated a lot of buzz in Israel.

Apply this understanding by...

- living as though you are Jesus' apostle sent into the world.

---

4. Don't take provision with you (Matt 10:9-10, Mark 6:8-9).
5. In each town, seek to find a welcoming place and let your peace rest on it if it is worthy; if not, let your peace return (Matt 10:11-13, Mark 6:10).
6. If a place will not welcome you, shake the dust off your feet as a sign of judgement (Matt 10:14-15, Mark 6:11).

The disciples' central task was to differentiate between people and cities, to find out who was welcoming the kingdom and who wasn't. The disciples were "angels" (or messengers) who were fulfilling the parable of the wheat and tares (Matt 13:24-30—Matthew is out of chronological order on this point). The people who rejected them were marked (bundled) for judgement (burning). They were not setting these towns and villages for some kind of heavenly judgement after Jesus returned; the judgment was coming in the near future. Beginning in A.D. 66 there were a series of conflicts between Israel and the Romans in which Rome destroyed numerous cities in Israel, starting with Jerusalem in A.D. 70. In the third revolt (Bar Kokhba) in A.D. 132-136, a second century historian reported that 50 fortified towns and 985 villages were destroyed. Jesus said regarding the towns that rejected the apostles, "It will be more tolerable for the land of Sodom and Gomorrah in the day of judgment than for that city" (Matt 10:15). Jesus' words were literally true; these towns were ruthlessly and cruelly razed by the Romans.

The sending out of the twelve can be isolated as a single episode within the life of Jesus, but it was also the beginning of a greater sending out. Later, He would send out the seventy; and ultimately, Jesus' followers would be sent out to take the gospel to the ends of the earth. Jesus instructed His twelve disciples in their current task with this greater mission in view.

The gist of Jesus' teaching regarding the twelve's greater mission (in Matt 10:5-42) was that they would be persecuted, but the Spirit would give them words to say. If Jesus was called Beelzebub, how much more would His apostles be defamed. Jesus' encouragement was to not be afraid, but to trust in Him. Their task was hard, but that is what followers of Jesus do; they do hard things, they give up everything to follow Him. For that they will be greatly rewarded.

We don't know much about how successful the twelve were in bringing the gospel of the kingdom to Israel, but we do know that it generated quite a bit of buzz. Herod heard about it and was concerned about who Jesus might be. He thought that He was John the Baptist raised from the dead (Mark 6:14).

APPLICATION

In a sense, each one of us are apostles of the kingdom. We are sent out to finish the mission that Jesus left to His disciples and the disciples have passed on to us. Too often we simply go about our daily lives without considering the greater calling that we have in the kingdom.

ACTIVITIES

1. Journal Time. Our lives here on earth are about much more than simply going about our daily tasks or leading a successful life in the world's eyes. We are to be like the apostles—sent out to share the good news of the kingdom. Spend some time thinking and praying about how God wants to use your life for the kingdom like He used the lives of the apostles. Then, in the space below. You can write your prayers or write your convictions on how God might be leading you.

Unit 4: Jesus Rejected

1. Parable of the Wheat and Tares. Read Matthew 13:24-30 and answer the following questions.

How were the disciples fulfilling this parable in the story covered in this lesson?_____
_____
_____
_____
_____

Who are the wheat?_____
_____
_____

Who are the tares?_____
_____
_____

What does bundling and burning mean?_____
_____
_____
_____
_____
_____

Lesson 4.4

EVALUATION

1. Jesus' closest disciples had been following Him since early in His Galilean ministry, but when did Jesus really start training them to be apostles? _____
_____

2. What does the word "apostle" mean?_____

3. When the twelve were sent out, what, in essence, was their task?_____
_____
_____

4. To whom were the twelve sent? _____
_____

5. What message were they to preach in the towns they went into? _____
_____

6. What were they to do if a town didn't welcome them?_____
_____

7. What did the apostles actions towards the unwelcoming town mean? _____
_____

LESSON 4.5

The Feeding of the 5,000

UNIT 4

THE STORY

Lesson Theme - Jesus didn't accept easy popularity; He wanted people who trusted Him.

In the context of the overall point of the passage, the feeding of the 5,000 almost fades into the background. Don't worry about that—there's a huge lesson in faith to be gleaned from the miracle, and we will see Jesus' teachings on this topic in Lesson 4.7. For the purposes of this lesson, the miracle of the feeding of the 5,000 was to set up Jesus' enormous popularity.

Do notice though, a couple of key features about the miracle. First, Jesus didn't just do it. He tossed the problem to Philip, to see what he'd do with it (John 6:5). We'll come back to this in the next lesson. Second, just notice the fact of the thing: Jesus fed a crowd of 5,000 men from five loaves and two fish.

Understanding the crowd's response is crucial to grasping what happened next. The crowd saw the sign, understood that Jesus was the prophesied prophet like Moses (cf. Deut 18:15, Acts 3:22, 7:37), and they wanted to make Him king, whether He wanted to be king or not (John 6:14-15).

Jesus withdrew up the mountain by Himself, and then at evening the disciples took a boat to cross the sea to Capernaum (John 6:15-17). A storm hit, and in the second miracle of the passage (a private one for the twelve) Jesus appeared, walking on water outside the boat (John 6:19). When the disciples received Him into the boat, they found themselves immediately at land (John 6:21). Walking on water was not the only part of

OVERVIEW

Jesus worked a miracle and became very popular for the wrong reasons. In order to continue on His mission without being encumbered by an army of 5,000 men trying to make Him king, Jesus challenged their spiritual dullness, offended them, and even drove away a number of His disciples as a result.

SOURCE MATERIAL

- **John 6:1-71**
- Matthew 14:13-33
- Mark 6:32-52
- Luke 9:10-17

this miracle. The feeding of the 5,000 took place near Bethsaida, at a location which was probably about six miles from Capernaum across the sea. The disciples had only rowed three or four miles when they met Jesus, and as soon as He got into the boat, they arrived at Capernaum—meaning that Jesus miraculously subtracted at least two miles from their journey.

Both the miracle of the feeding of the 5,000 and Jesus' miraculous trip to Capernaum though, were a set-up for what happened next. The people who wanted to make Jesus king got on boats and came to find Him (John 6:24). They questioned Him about His arrival in Capernaum, and He immediately shifted the conversation to talk about the state of their hearts. He told them they didn't really get the point of the sign; they were just chasing earthly food when they

Unit 4: Jesus Rejected

OBJECTIVES

Feel...

- interested that there is such a thing as a godly time, place, and way to offend someone.
- perhaps some anxiety about the moral quality of his own popularity.

Understand...

- that Jesus became very popular because of the miracle of the feeding of the 5,000.
- that the popularity was not helpful to Jesus' mission, so He got rid of it by deliberately giving offense to people who liked Him for the wrong reasons.
- that Jesus did not explain Himself to His disciples and as a result, lost many of them too.
- that the twelve stayed, not because they understood what Jesus was saying, but because they trusted who He was.

Apply this understanding by...

- considering your own popularity (such as it may be) and understanding whether in your case, your popularity is helpful or harmful.
- considering whether you view Jesus more like the crowds did (someone to give you what you want) or like the disciples did (hard to understand, but the Lord who does things His own way).
- recognizing that sometimes it's necessary to trust God even without understanding what He is doing.

should have been seeking for all that Jesus could give them (John 6:26-27). The people still didn't understand what Jesus was saying and responded by asking how they could do miracles too (this is what "works of God" [John 6:28] means in context). Jesus turned their question back on them by telling them that the only miracle they needed was to believe in Him (John 6:29). They asked Him what sign He would do so they could believe in Him—and hinted strongly that producing bread from heaven like Moses had would be a good one. (This is how you can tell they were still just looking for a free lunch. If all they needed was a miraculous production of a meal, didn't Jesus just do that yesterday? But no, they wanted to see it again, and *then* they would believe. Riiiiight.) Jesus responded that Moses didn't give them bread from heaven, but the Father gives the *real* bread that comes down and gives life to the world (John 6:32-33). In Greek, "he who comes" and "that which comes" are the same expression, so they heard "that which comes down from heaven," still thinking that He was talking about literal bread...which made Jesus' next response a rude shock. "I am the bread of life," Jesus said (John 6:35).

They complained about Him at this point, because Jesus was claiming to have come down from heaven, and yet they knew His parents (John 6:41-42). In their minds, He was claiming the impossible.

Jesus rebuked them for grumbling among themselves. He then explained that no one could believe in Him without first being drawn by the Father which entailed learning from the Father *first*. Everyone who had heard the Father, who had learned from the Father, came to Jesus, and Jesus (He said it again!) was the bread of life. Not like manna—all the people who ate manna were long dead—but anyone who ate this bread would live forever. And the bread He was talking about, Jesus said, was His own flesh that He

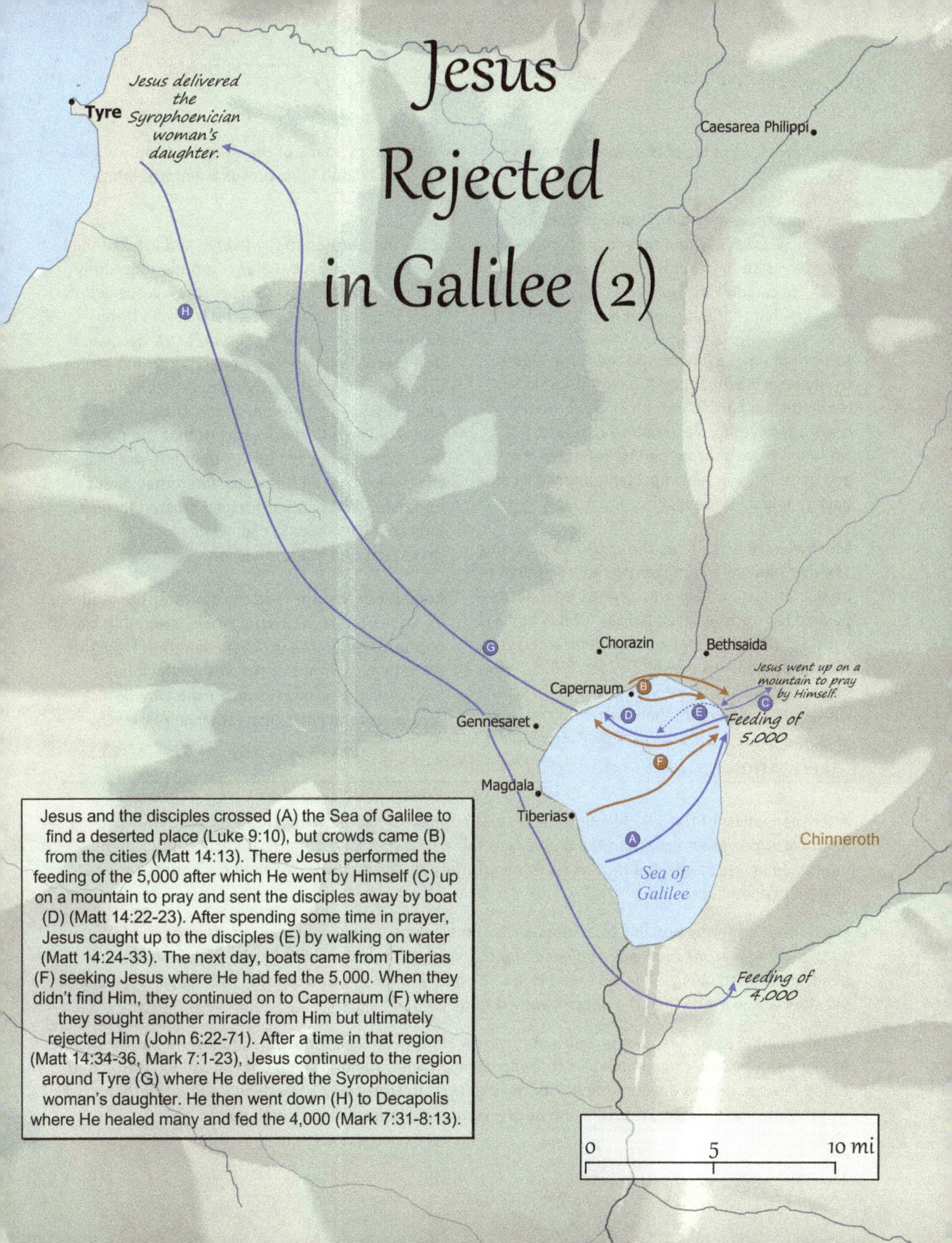

Unit 4: Jesus Rejected

would give for the life of the world (John 6:43-51).

Now they *knew* they didn't quite understand what He was saying, and they fought amongst themselves about what He could mean (John 6:52). He couldn't possibly be talking about cannibalism, but that's sure what it sounded like.

Jesus didn't make it easier on them. He didn't clarify what He meant by the metaphor; in fact, He hit it even harder. In John 6:53-58, He didn't really say anything He hadn't said before, but He said it more sharply, and He repeated it over and over. This is really important, and we'll come back to it in a moment.

Meanwhile, it wasn't just the crowd complaining. The disciples were complaining that they didn't understand what Jesus was saying either. Jesus pushed His disciples even harder. "If this bothers you," Jesus said, "What will you think when you see Me ascend into heaven?" (John 6:62*). He went on to insist that He was giving them life in His words, but some of them just didn't believe.

At this point, many of the disciples simply walked away and didn't follow Jesus anymore (John 6:66).

Jesus then turned to the twelve and asked if they wanted to leave too. Peter responded that they had nowhere else to go—they knew Jesus' words were life, and that He was the Messiah (John 6:68-69). Notice that Peter *didn't* say, "No, we don't want to leave—we understand what You're driving at." The twelve didn't understand what Jesus was saying here any better than anybody else did. The difference was not that the twelve understood while the others didn't. It was that the twelve trusted Him even when they didn't understand. The other disciples trusted Jesus as long as things made sense; when things didn't make sense anymore, they left.

Remember that this was the day after the feeding of the 5,000, when the crowd wanted to kidnap Jesus and make Him king, whether He wanted to be king or not. Jesus was wildly popular, but for all the wrong reasons—the crowds just wanted Him to keep giving them a free lunch.

APPLICATION

After the feeding of the 5,000 fanboys, Jesus was popular for all the wrong reasons. He didn't do anything wrong (obviously), but the crowds got the wrong message from His miracle. They weren't interested in Jesus and what He was really about; they just wanted Him for their own purposes—to give them a free lunch.

Of course it's entirely possible to be popular for doing wrong things, but you can also be popular for all the wrong reasons *even when you're doing the right thing*. Jesus didn't let the popularity go to His head; He kept on being who God called Him to be and doing what God called Him to do, and He didn't get sidetracked even when the people wanted to make Him king.

At this point in Jesus' life, part of God's purpose for Him was to call some of His followers out for their wrong motives and "clean house," so that the ones left were the ones who understood what God had called Jesus to be and do. Sometimes God may call you to stop doing something good, something that was making you popular. Trust Him and obey—your real friends will stick with you.

Lesson 4.5

This does not mean that popularity is bad in itself. Remember that in growing up, "Jesus increased in wisdom and stature, and in favor with God and men" (Luke 2:52). Having people's favor can be a gift from God and a good thing or it can be an absolute disaster. Think about the people who have favor toward you: does their favor help you and move you closer to God, or does it hurt you and move you further away?

ACTIVITIES

1. Journal Time: Trusting God. The twelve disciples chose to trust Jesus even though they didn't understand everything He was saying. Think of a time in the past or of a current situation where you didn't understand what God was doing. In the space below, write about this situation and, if God later made His purposes clear to you, write about that too. Then write a prayer to God, asking Him to help you trust Him even when you don't understand.

Unit 4: Jesus Rejected

2. Personal Reflection: Who Are You in the Story? Reflect carefully on your own life. Are you like the many who just wanted a free lunch? Do you follow Jesus because you know He'll do good things for you if you do? Or are you like the 12 who trusted Jesus even though they didn't understand exactly what was going on? Maybe you respond to Jesus differently at different times. Write your thoughts below.

Lesson 4.5

EVALUATION

1. How did Jesus set up the feeding of the 5,000? _____
_____
_____

2. How much food was left over? _____

3. How did the crowd respond? _____

4. What did Jesus do about that response? _____

5. Where did the feeding take place, and where did the crowd catch up to Jesus? _____
_____

6. How did Jesus respond to the crowd when they caught up to Him? _____
_____

7. What did Jesus do when the crowd misunderstood Him? _____
_____

8. Why didn't Jesus explain Himself at least to His disciples? _____
_____
_____

LESSON 4.6

Miraculous Healings and the Feeding of the 4,000

UNIT 4

THE STORY

Lesson Theme - Jesus built the disciples' faith in multiple areas.

The disciples already had faith for healing and casting out demons (see Matt 10:1, Mark 6:7-13). Jesus had sent them out two-by-two, and they had been successful. But their faith was lacking in other areas, and Jesus set out to expand it.

Matthew, Mark and John all talk about this portion of Jesus' ministry at different levels of detail, but for this lesson we'll mainly follow Matthew's account. The events of Matthew 14:34-15:20 all took place on the same day as the events of John 6 that were the focus of the previous lesson, the day after the feeding of the 5,000.

Jesus was famous at this point in His ministry and known for healing. When He landed in Gennesaret (the region northwest of the Sea of Galilee where Capernaum was found), the people recognized Him and sent out word to gather the sick. Many of them just touched the hem of His robe, and that was enough to perfectly heal them (Matt 14:35-36).

Meanwhile, Pharisees and scribes from Jerusalem (who were probably in Galilee for the purpose of observing Jesus) also heard that Jesus was there, and came to watch. At some point during all this, Jesus' disciples got hungry and ate—and they continued their habit of annoying the Pharisees by eating without washing their hands. Of course, the Pharisees noticed this right away and brought it to Jesus' attention. "Why

OVERVIEW

Jesus continued to build the disciples' faith in different areas: their treatment of the religious leaders, their understanding of praying in faith, and their trust for God's provision.

SOURCE MATERIAL

- **Matthew 14:34-15:39**
- Mark 6:53-8:9
- John 7:1

do Your disciples break our ancient traditions?" (Matt 15:2*) they wanted to know.

The last time the Pharisees had this conversation with Jesus, He just pointed out that it was necessary to maintain a sense of proportion about these things (see Lesson 3.5, Luke 6:1-5). This time though, Jesus went after the Pharisees: "Why do you break *God's commandment* because of your ancient tradition?" (Matt 15:3*).

Of course the Pharisees would deny that they did any such thing, but Jesus had an example ready. In order to understand the point Jesus made here, you need to understand three pieces of background information:

- In Jesus' society, there were no nursing homes and no Social Security or other retirement accounts. When people got too old to work to support themselves, they relied on their children to care for them in their old age. So a critical part of obeying the com-

Unit 4: Jesus Rejected

OBJECTIVES

Feel...

- perhaps some tension and anxiety over asking God for big things.
- a sense of anticipation to see what God is going to do when he asks God for these big things.
- determination to keep asking until God does it.

Understand...

- the cultural factors that made Jesus' critique of the Pharisees so powerful.
- that Jesus confronted the Pharisees on their use of substitute sources of purity rather than purity of the heart.
- that substitute sources of purity are often good things in themselves, but they don't really work as a substitute for a right heart.
- that just because the leaders were wrong, didn't mean it was Jesus' job to reform them.
- that God loves persistence in prayer.
- that God provides for our needs in any situation He calls us into.

Apply this understanding by...

- thinking about what substitute sources of purity you tend to rely on rather than dealing with the real issues in your heart.
- choosing one of the bigger problems in your life right now, thinking through what it would look like for God's will to be done in that situation, and then stepping out in faith to pray for that—no matter how ridiculous the request might be—and praying consistently for it until God answers.

mand to honor your father and mother was to take care of them when they got old.

- There was a legitimate category in the Old Testament Law of things that are "Corban"—devoted to God. These were things that could not be immediately delivered to the temple treasury because of distance or other issues, but they were considered to be God's property even though they temporarily remained in the individual's possession.
- The Pharisees were *the* big advocates of purity before God in that culture. They were famous for being meticulous about being pure.

Although the Corban law was legitimate for certain cases, the Pharisees applied it in a way that would give people permission to break the fifth commandment. If a person were to say, "Anything I might have used to support my parents is devoted to God," then according to the Pharisees, he *was not allowed* to give anything to Mom and Dad, because all that stuff now belonged to God. This was never the intent of the original Corban laws and obviously violated God's Law, but it was the Pharisees' tradition to allow it.

Jesus condemned their tradition and quoted Isaiah 29:13, which was originally spoken to Israel during a time of desperate spiritual decline. In effect, Jesus was saying, "You Pharisees and scribes are as bad off as Israel was back then"—and back then, God carried the whole nation off into the Babylonian captivity. Jesus was saying the Pharisees were in that much spiritual danger, and they couldn't even see it (Matt 15:3-10).

Then, to make matters "worse," Jesus called the whole crowd over and said, "Listen up, everybody! Make sure you get this. It's not what you put into your mouth that makes you impure; it's what comes out of your mouth that makes you impure" (Matt 10:11*). Of course the Pharisees were deeply offended—what He just said was that His disciples, defying the tradition, were fine, but the Pharisees were impure because they repeated the tradition and defied God's Law.

At this point, the disciples came to Jesus, concerned. "Do You know that the Pharisees were offended when they heard this?" (Matt 15:12). It was one thing to annoy the Pharisees by not washing their hands, but it was another thing entirely to accuse the *Pharisees* of *impurity*. In public! Those were fighting words.

Jesus responded with two illustrations found in Matthew 15:13-14. It's very important that Jesus said to leave the Pharisees alone. He did not say, "These guys are wrong and they're doing work that God never said to do, so go on a crusade against them and tell everybody why they're wrong." No. The Pharisees were wrong, and their work was not for God, and God was not in it—so the disciples were to *leave them alone* (Matt 15:14).

Then Peter asked Jesus to explain the parable He had told the crowd, and Jesus explained it very simply (Matt 15:17-20). What goes into the mouth is eventually eliminated from the body; that doesn't make anyone impure before God. But what people say comes from their hearts, so evil speech comes from an evil heart, and these things do make a person impure before God.

From here, Jesus went up into the area around Tyre and Sidon, where a Canaanite woman kept following Him around, asking Him to cast a demon out of her daughter (Matt 15:21-22). Jesus ignored her, but it got so annoying that His disciples finally asked Him to send her away. When Jesus did finally engage the woman, He told her that He was sent to Israel (Matt 15:24). She continued to beg Him for help, but He said that it's not good to take the children's food and throw it to the dogs. Jesus' comment was offensive, but also spoke to the point He made earlier: He was sent to Israel, not to the Gentiles. The woman played off His illustration and carried it one step further. "Sure," she said. "You don't give the children's food to the dogs, but the dogs do get the scraps that fall off their master's table" (Matt 15:27*). Immediately, Jesus commended the woman's faith and healed her daughter (Matt 15:28).

Why did Jesus commend her faith? Because she believed He could and would heal; because she didn't stop asking until He did; and because rather than being offended by Him, she accepted His interpretation of events and worked within it.

From Tyre and Sidon, Jesus went back down past Galilee and up onto a mountain, and again He healed the people who came to Him: lame, blind, mute, maimed, and many others (Matt 15:29-30). All this was pretty normal for His disciples by now, but then Jesus upped the ante. It was the same situation as the feeding of the 5,000 all over again, but it was a little more serious now. Last time, they *could* have sent the crowd away, but this time it was too late. The crowd had been following Jesus for three days. Not only were they completely out of food, they might not have made it back to town where they could get some (Matt 15:32).

The disciples panicked. They had no idea where all that bread was going to come from (Matt 15:33). Jesus asked them what food they had. This time they had more than last time (seven loaves and a few fish). Jesus did exactly the same

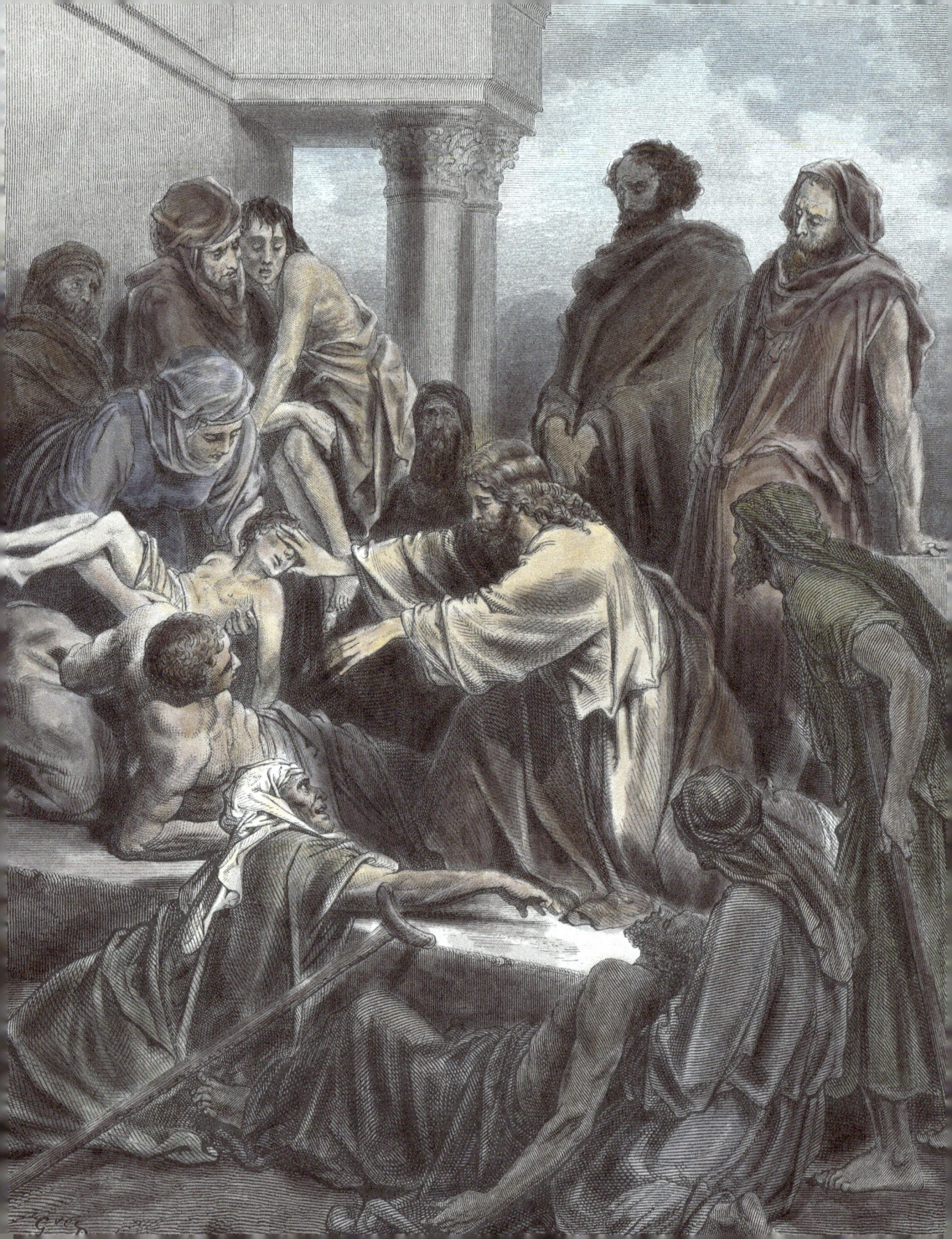

Lesson 4.6

thing as He did before: He had the disciples tell the people to sit down, He gave thanks for the food, and He distributed it to His disciples to distribute in turn to the crowd. And again, there were leftovers—seven baskets (Matt 15:37).

After feeding the crowd, Jesus sent them away (possibly to discourage the "let's make Him king" movement from getting started again), and took a boat to Magdala (another port at the western-most edge of the Sea of Galilee).

APPLICATION

The big lesson here is about faith. The disciples had healed all kinds of diseases and cast out demons in Jesus' name; we would think of them as men of faith already. But when the important people (Pharisees) were offended at what Jesus said, the disciples were concerned. Jesus taught them not to worry about it, to just leave them alone and keep doing the right thing. We ought to do the same. There's a great temptation to go after everything that seems wrong, but often the right thing to do is let those people go, and just do the work yourself rather than trying to correct them.

The Canaanite woman gives another lesson in faith—she kept asking, even when Jesus ignored her, even when Jesus told her He was not really that interested. She just accepted His interpretation of the situation, and kept asking anyhow. This kind of perseverance requires faith because when you're in that situation, you look and feel like an idiot. "God is not responding; why would I keep asking? He seems to be saying no; why would I keep asking? I'm just looking like an idiot here." Jesus said that's what great faith looks like.

Finally, in the feeding of the 4,000, Jesus was teaching the disciples to trust God for provision in the wilderness, just like Israel once had to learn. Jesus had done this lesson before, but it took Israel more than once to learn it too. Here the application is simple: if God gets you into a situation, He will care for you though it.

ACTIVITIES

1. Purity Before God. The Pharisees had a long list of ways to maintain purity before God. Washing hands before eating was just one of them. Jesus told the disciples that external cleanliness isn't how purity really works; it's about what is in the heart. We might not have the same list that the Pharisees had, but in our culture, we have our own set of traditions that we use instead of really addressing the sins in our hearts (see Matt 14:19 for a handy list). In the space below, brainstorm a list of the things people use as substitute sources of purity rather than dealing with their sin. _____

_____

_____

Unit 4: Jesus Rejected

(continued)

2. A Big, Stupid Prayer. Think about some of the problems you face in your life. In the Lord's Prayer, Jesus said, "Thy kingdom come; Thy will be done on earth as it is in heaven." What would it look like for God's kingdom to break out right there in the middle of your biggest problem? In the space below, write a prayer asking God's kingdom to come in the midst of your problem. It can feel like a stupid thing to pray for, but Jesus praised the Canaanite woman for taking her big request and just asking over and over until He did it.

Lesson 4.6

EVALUATION

1. What were the Pharisees known for? _____

2. How did old people get taken care of in Jesus' society? Nursing homes? Social Security payments?
_____

3. What tradition of the Pharisees did Jesus criticize? _____
_____

4. Why did Jesus criticize the Pharisees' tradition? _____
_____

5. Did Jesus intend for the disciples to go off on an anti-Pharisee crusade? _____
_____
_____

6. What was the point Jesus was making to the crowd? _____
_____

7. Why did Jesus say that the Canaanite woman had great faith? _____
_____

8. Compare and contrast the feedings of the 5,000 and the 4,000. What was the same? What was different? _____
_____
_____
_____
_____

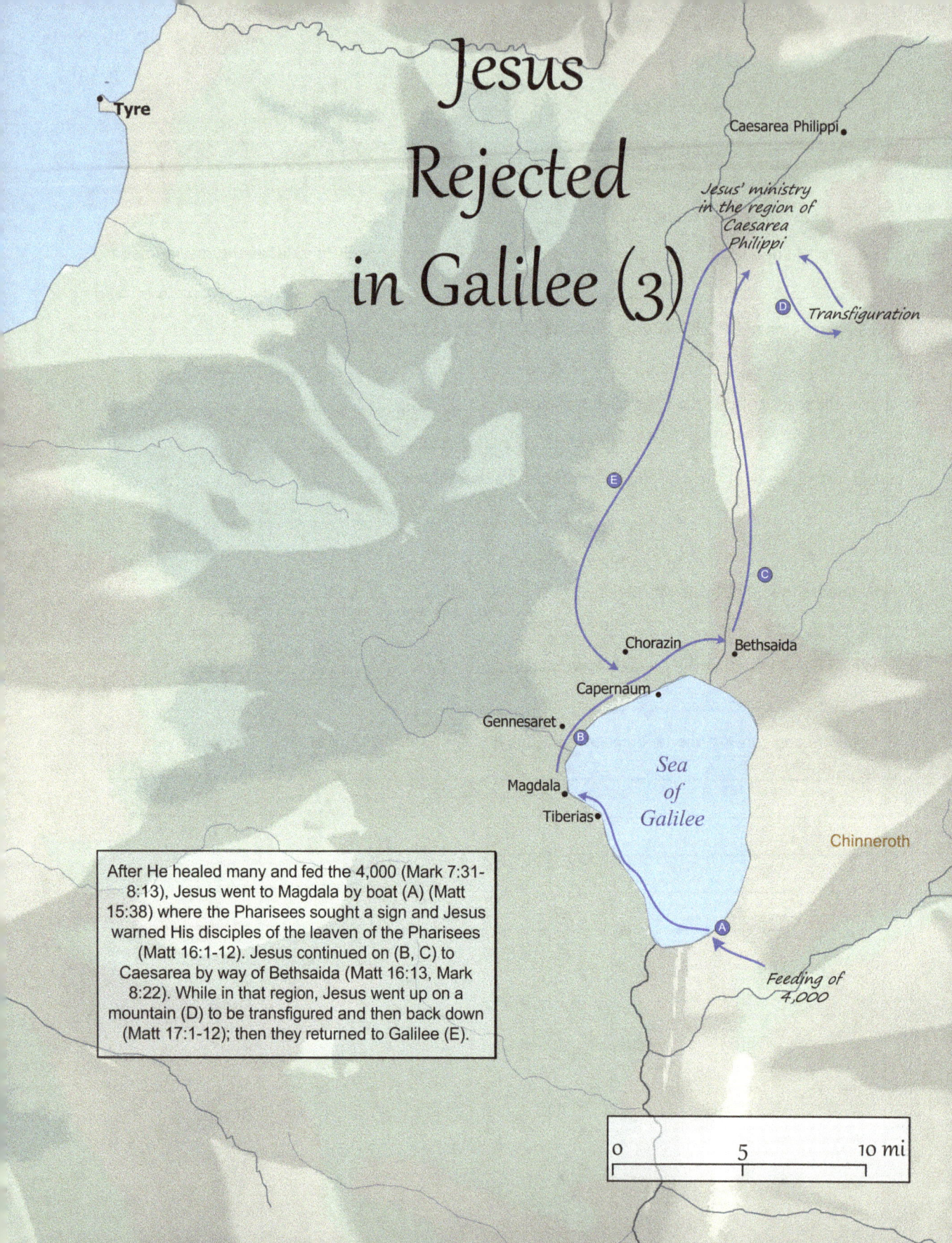

LESSON 4.7

The Leaven of the Pharisees

UNIT 4

THE STORY

Lesson Theme - Jesus can provide for our needs. The focus of this lesson is a little conversation in which Jesus warned the disciples about the religious leaders and, at the same time, connected the dots that allowed them to learn a lesson about the Father's provision.

After the feeding of the 4,000, Jesus took a boat to Magdala (some translations say Magadan, a different name for the same place), the westernmost port on the Sea of Galilee.

There He was accosted by the Pharisees and Sadducees, who challenged Him to produce a sign from heaven (Matt 16:1). The timing of their request is a big deal here. Jesus had just attacked the Pharisees for using their tradition to break the Law of God (see Matt 15:3-6, Lesson 4.6). The Pharisees' traditions were absolutely revered, and their natural response to Jesus' attack would've been something along the lines of, "Who do *you* think you are to attack our ancient traditions?" This was the way they framed it, "If you're so great, Jesus of Nazareth, if you speak for God, then prove it—show us a sign from God!" (Matt 16:1*).

Jesus didn't take the bait. He'd been healing the sick, making the lame walk, the blind see, the deaf hear, casting out demons, feeding first 5,000 people, then 4,000 more miraculously. If that wasn't enough, one more miraculous sign was certainly not going to convince them. Instead, He rebuked their inability to understand the signs that were right in front of them (Matt 16:2-4). They could tell when it was going to rain,

OVERVIEW

Jesus had been training His disciples to trust the Father for provision, but they hadn't really gotten the message. In this lesson, Jesus connected the dots for them.

SOURCE MATERIAL

- **Matthew 15:39-16:12**
- Mark 8:10-21

but they couldn't tell when the Messiah had come.

Regarding the bit about predicting the weather based on the red sky, there's an old proverb in English: "Red sky at morning, sailors take warning; red sky at night, sailors' delight." As with much old weather lore, there is a scientific basis for this proverb.

Because they were a wicked and adulterous generation, Jesus would give them no sign except the sign of the prophet Jonah (Matt 16:4). Of course He was speaking in riddles again, and they wouldn't understand it. Jonah was "dead" for three days inside the fish that swallowed him and then "rose from the dead" when the fish spat him out. Even the disciples didn't understand until after the resurrection. With that riddle, Jesus left the religious leaders.

After He had withdrawn with His disciples, Jesus said, "Take heed and beware of the leaven of the Pharisees and Sadducees" (Matt 15:6). Jesus was constantly talking in metaphors and parables, and of course His meaning was very often not

Unit 4: Jesus Rejected

OBJECTIVES

Feel...

- security that the Father will take care of you in whatever He leads you into.
- concern about absorbing respectable but false ideas about God and the world.

Understand...

- that the Pharisees had seen plenty of signs throughout Jesus' ministry.
- that the Pharisees' request for a sign was not sincere; a sign wasn't going to convince them.
- the connection between the feeding of the 5,000, the feeding of the 4,000, and the conversation that takes place in Matthew 16:8-11.
- that the Pharisees were absolutely respectable in their society.

Apply this understanding by...

- considering what sort of things you worry about and committing them to God.
- thinking through what sort of false teachers today might be like the Pharisees.

obvious. So the disciples huddled up and tried to figure it out. Their conclusion was that He was rebuking them for forgetting to bring some bread with them when they crossed the sea (Matt 16:7).

Knowing what they had concluded, Jesus rebuked them for their lack of faith, reminding them of the feeding of the 5,000 and all its leftovers and the feeding of the 4,000 and all its leftovers (Matt 16:8-11). Jesus was not talking about bread, but He also didn't explain what He was talking about; He just repeated what He had said before. He wanted the disciples to figure it out.

With the bread explanation off the table, they did figure it out (Matt 16:12). But why did Jesus *need* to warn them against the doctrine of the Pharisees and Sadducees? Recall that the disciples were concerned when Jesus offended the Pharisees just a little earlier (Matt 15:12, Lesson 4.6). The disciples still had a higher regard for the Pharisees than they really should have; if they saw the Pharisees the way Jesus did, they wouldn't have been worried about offending them. So Jesus was prompting them to reconsider their respect for the Pharisees.

APPLICATION

Jesus taught the disciples two lessons here, both of them readily applicable.

First, whatever the Father leads you into, the Father will supply. Stuck in the desert with thousands of people and no food? If the Father led you there, don't worry about it. Of course, this assumes *that we are following the Father's leading*. If we are going our own way, we can't expect God to finance the trip. So the practical application is twofold: first, follow the Father's leading, and second, trust Him to provide.

The other lesson has to do with having respect for the wrong people. The disciples had already begun following Jesus' example of irritating the Pharisees by breaking their traditions, but they were concerned when Jesus *really* offended them. They still had enough regard for the Pharisees that Jesus needed to warn them about the Pharisees' doctrine. People who oppose Jesus are not just people we shouldn't pay attention to—we are free to just leave them alone; but we also need to be careful not to unwittingly assimilate their teaching.

ACTIVITIES

1. Worrying about Following God's Leading. One of the major lessons in this passage is to trust God to provide for your needs wherever He leads you. Unlike people in Jesus' day, you probably don't have to worry about starving in the desert before you can reach the next town. In the space below, answer the following questions.

What are some worries you face or could see yourself facing in the future? _____

_____
_____
_____
_____

What might God ask you to do, and what might you worry about when you step out to do it? _____

_____
_____
_____
_____

2. The Teaching of the Pharisees and Sadducees. While most Christians are not in particular danger today of believing what the Pharisees taught 2,000 years ago, we still have false teachers today. Answer the following questions.

Name some false teachers and false teachings that happen today. _____

_____
_____
_____
_____
_____
_____

Unit 4: Jesus Rejected

How are we in danger of absorbing this teaching? _____

_____

_____

_____

_____

_____

How can we protect ourselves from absorbing this false teaching? _____

_____

_____

_____

_____

_____

_____

_____

_____

_____

EVALUATION

1. How did people feel about the Pharisees in Jesus' time? _____
_____

2. Why did the Pharisees ask Jesus for a sign? _____
_____
_____

3. Why did Jesus refuse to give them a sign? _____
_____
_____
_____

4. What one sign did Jesus offer? _____
_____

5. Why did Jesus call His death and resurrection "the sign of the prophet Jonah"? _____
_____
_____

6. Why did Jesus need to warn His disciples about the Pharisees' teaching? _____
_____
_____
_____

7. Why did the disciples think Jesus was talking about them forgetting bread? _____
_____
_____
_____

8. How did Jesus correct them? _____
_____
_____

LESSON 4.8

The Transfiguration: Peter Learned About the Path to Glory

UNIT 4

THE STORY

Lesson Theme - The path to glory goes through suffering.
Before you read this lesson, answer questions 1 and 2 in the activity called **Journal Time: View of Trials** at the end of the lesson.

The main point of this lesson is that one must pass through suffering in order to get to glory. More specifically, Jesus had to go through death before He could be seated at the right hand of God. But this was not only true of Jesus; it is true of every disciple as well. You want to identify with Peter and walk through his experiences in this passage in order to understand the relationship between suffering and glory.

Jesus' next step in training the disciples was to teach them what it meant to be the Messiah and what it meant to be a follower of the Messiah. On this occasion, Jesus asked His disciples, "Who do men say that I, the Son of Man, am?" (Matt 16:13). By this time, Jesus had made His way around Galilee and Judea several times healing the sick, casting out demons, and raising the dead—generally crushing the head of evil and challenging the established authorities. He had a reputation, and people knew that He was someone important. The disciples responded with the list that represented popular consensus on Jesus, "Some say John the Baptist..." (Matt 16:14). This was a popular answer; John the Baptist had been killed unjustly, and Jesus preached the same message that John had. We know that Herod, at least, thought that Jesus was John the Baptist returned. In addition, several legendary proph-

OVERVIEW

Peter was in tune with the Father and was able to boldly say that Jesus was the "Messiah, the Son of the living God" (Matt 16:16, NIV). But he didn't get the principle of baptism: that true life came through death. When Jesus told His disciples that He must suffer and die, Peter rebuked Him and then received a harsh rebuke from Jesus. Jesus taught them that the way of the cross was the way of discipleship and then gave His three closest disciples a foretaste of what His glory would look like.

SOURCE MATERIAL

- Matthew 16:13-17:13

ets were often brought up, probably because of the similarity between Jesus' message and theirs. All of these answers were partially true in a sense; Jesus was like a new John the Baptist, a new Elijah or a new Jeremiah. But none of these answers got at the heart of who Jesus was.

Jesus then asked His disciples, "But who do you say that I am?" (Matt 16:15). Peter, being the boldest of the disciples, answered confidently, "You are the Messiah, the Son of the living God" (Matt 16:16, NIV).

He nailed it—Jesus was God's son, the Messiah of God. And Jesus praised Peter for his correct answer. This answer wasn't something that Peter could just *come up with*—it was revealed to him by the Father in heaven (Matt 16:17). Peter was

Unit 4: Jesus Rejected

OBJECTIVES

Feel...

- frustration that Peter did not understand that the Messiah *must* suffer.
- excitement at the hopeful glimpse of the future in the Transfiguration.
- a sobriety of mind in understanding that suffering precedes glory.

Understand...

- that Jesus' identity as the Son of God was revealed to Peter by the Father.
- that the Messiah *had to* suffer because suffering always precedes glory.
- that the principle of baptism is that suffering always precedes glory.
- that Peter's rebuke of Jesus resulted from a fundamental misunderstanding of how the world works and what Jesus came to do.
- that the Transfiguration was an "outside of time" glimpse into the kingdom.
- that Peter wanted to build houses for Jesus, Elijah and Moses because he wanted to capture the kingdom before any suffering.

Apply this understanding by...

- coming to grips with your call to pass through suffering to receive glory.

hearing from God. Armed with this truth, Peter, a small stone (the meaning of *petros* in Greek), would be the a big rock on which Christ would build His Church (Matt 16:18-19). Peter would have real power to bring the heavenly kingdom to earth.

Peter got that Jesus was the Messiah, but he didn't understand what it meant to be the Messiah. "From that time Jesus began to show to His disciples that He must go to Jerusalem, and suffer many things from the elders and chief priests and scribes, and be killed, and be raised the third day" (Matt 16:21). Jesus *had to* suffer, not, Jesus *would* suffer. There was something inevitable about Jesus' suffering, as though it was required, because it was. For God to express love in a world of suffering and sin, He *had to* enter into that suffering and sin. If Jesus simply became man, set up a kingdom and was exalted to the right hand of God without passing through death, He would've missed what it means to be human; He would have left man in his sin without hope; He would have been a bad king. The path to glory *always* goes through death in God's world.

This was not a new concept; the disciples should've known that this is how the world works. The world operates on the principle of baptism; death leads to resurrection life, true life, and there is no shortcut. The world was covered with water before the land came to life and passed underwater again at the first new creation: Noah's flood. Israel passed through the Red Sea before being constituted as a nation under Moses on the other side. Jesus' own baptism spoke of His greater baptism still to come: His death and resurrection. "He *must*... be killed, and be raised the third day" (Matt 16:21, emphasis added).

But the disciples didn't get it, especially not Peter. The one who had just called Jesus the "Son of the living God" now rebuked the Messiah. "Never Lord... This shall never happen to you!" (Matt 16:22, NIV). The word for rebuke here is the same word that is used to describe what Jesus was doing when He cast out or rebuked a demon. This was a serious confrontation by Peter, but far outside an understanding of how God's world works. As a result, Jesus, who had just praised Peter for hearing from the Father, rebuked Him as an agent of Satan! A moment ago, Jesus called him a "rock" on whom the Church would be built; now He called him a "stumbling block" (Matt 16:23, NIV). This was something that Jesus knew His disciples *had to* understand in order to be His apostles; anyone who wants to be a disciple of Jesus has to follow in His footsteps: he has to pass through suffering to attain glory.

So Jesus explained it them, "If anyone desires to come after Me, let him deny himself, and take up his cross, and follow Me" (Matt 16:24). In other words, in order to gain true life, you must let go of life, and whoever holds on to life will never have it. One day, Jesus is going to return to reward each person according to what they have done (Matt 16:27), and the ones who have let go of everything will get the greatest reward.

This discussion between Jesus and His disciples ended in a somewhat odd fashion. Jesus made the statement, "Assuredly, I say to you, there are some standing here who shall not taste death till they see the Son of Man coming in His kingdom" (Matt 16:28). "*Some*, why would Jesus say *some*?" His disciples probably asked themselves. After all, Jesus had just said that *all* of His disciples would have to give up their lives. Would some make it into the kingdom without passing through death? That seemed to contradict what Jesus had just said.

The answer lies in the next narrative in Matthew: the Transfiguration (Matt 17:1-13). It is easy to miss the connection here with a chapter break in between, but Matthew draws our attention to the connection by saying, "Now after six days..." (Matt 17:1). Six days later, Peter, James and John went up on a mountain with Jesus where He did *come in His kingdom* (Matt 16:28). Before the eyes of these three disciples, Jesus appeared *outside of time*; it was as though they got a glimpse into the future with Jesus, in glorified body, standing with a glorified Moses and Elijah.

From Peter's perspective, the time had come; the kingdom was here. He suggested they build some houses and capture this moment forever (Matt 17:4). And just then, God spoke from heaven repeating what He spoke over Jesus at His baptism and adding a command for the disciples: "Hear Him!" (Matt 17:5). By the time the disciples had recovered from the power of God's voice, everything had returned to normal. They had seen Jesus come in His kingdom, but that time had not yet come; He had to pass through death first.

Jesus instructed them not to tell anyone what they had seen until after His resurrection (Matt 17:9). Death had to come before resurrection and glory. These disciples got a foretaste of that glory, one that would bring hope to countless followers of Christ; but for now, even though they didn't really grasp its full meaning, this experience was theirs to keep.

APPLICATION

Like Jesus and His disciples, we all must pass through suffering in order to find glory. Your application from this lesson is to get used to that idea, or even start to be okay with it. Pray to God and tell Him that you understand that suffering is on the path to glory and you are okay with that. Often, God will give us a foretaste of glory in this life after we have gone through suffering, but sometimes we will never find glory until we meet Christ face-to-face and receive our reward from Him.

Unit 4: Jesus Rejected

ACTIVITIES

1. Journal Time: View of Trials. Before this lesson, spend some time writing in space below about questions 1 and 2. After this lesson, answer questions 3 and 4.

1. Do you generally view trials/difficulties as good or bad things? Explain your answer._____
_____
_____
_____
_____
_____

2. Describe a difficult experience you've had or are currently having. Did or do you think of this particular experience as a good or bad thing?_____
_____
_____
_____
_____
_____

3. What did Jesus teach about difficulties or trials? How does He want us to think of our trials?_____
_____
_____
_____

3. Look back at the difficult experience you wrote about at the beginning of this lesson. How does what Jesus taught about trials change the way you think about this experience?_____
_____
_____
_____
_____
_____

2. Write a Short Story. Jesus taught that a person must go through a cross experience, a genuine trial, before being glorified. Our culture tells us, "You are great; you can do anything you set your mind to and easily overcome any obstacle." Your job is to write two different short stories, a self-made hero story (the one our culture tells us is true) and a way-of-the-cross story (the one Jesus says is true). Some instructions are given below.

- Each story should be about one page long, but the way-of-the-cross story will be slightly longer than the self-made hero story.
- In both stories, the basic plot is: a knight conquers a dragon to rescue the princess and marry her.
- In the first story, the knight is so awesome that he is able to defeat the dragon with no problem. Every step of the way confirms his awesomeness.
- In the second story, the knight goes through some terrible ordeal either before facing the dragon that makes him capable of defeating the dragon, or during the process of defeating the dragon. He must find help outside of himself, either by bringing to life a truth that he has learned from someone else but never understood before, or by depending on something outside of himself to make it through the ordeal. In either case, he must sustain some kind of injury in the process of defeating the dragon.

First Story (self-made hero story):

Unit 4: Jesus Rejected

Second Story (way-of-the-cross story):

EVALUATION

1. How did Peter know that Jesus was the Messiah, the Son of God? _____

2. Why did Jesus have to suffer and die? _____

3. What biblical symbol teaches us that suffering precedes glory? _____

4. Why did Jesus respond so sharply to Peter's rebuke? _____

5. What was the Transfiguration demonstrating to the disciples who were there? _____

6. Why did Peter want to build houses for Jesus, Moses and Elijah at the Transfiguration, and what did this reveal about him? _____

LESSON 4.9

Jesus Taught the Disciples About Greatness

THE STORY

Lesson Theme - The disciples took their first trip through failure and learned about greatness. This lesson is a small-scale outworking of the principle from the last lesson: the path to glory comes through suffering. Specifically, in this lesson, the path to greatness for the disciples passed through failure.

In Lesson 4.3 we learned how Jesus began to train His disciples' faith. Faith is the currency, the lifeblood, of the kingdom of God. Being a disciple does not automatically give one great faith. Faith often comes from experience. Failure is part of the path to greater faith and therefore, greater glory. In this lesson, we will see how the disciples learned these very things.

By this time in Jesus' ministry, the twelve disciples had been sent out two-by-two and had cast out demons and healed the sick. At some point during this time, a demonized boy was brought to the disciples to be healed, but they were unable to heal him (Matt 17:14-16). Now that Jesus had come to the town, the boy was presented to Him. With a simple rebuke, the demon came out of the boy and he was healed (Matt 17:18).

The disciples came to Jesus privately and asked why they were unable to cast the demon out. Jesus' answer was not that they had said the wrong words or performed the wrong ritual. The problem was that they lacked faith (Matt 17:20). We learned earlier that faith is not simply an on or off kind of thing; rather, you can have more or less of it. The disciples needed more faith,

OVERVIEW

When the disciples failed to cast out a demon, Jesus taught them about faith and prayer. Their failure drove home the point better than success ever could have. As they continued on, Jesus taught them that true greatness would require them to humble themselves and become like little children, which would mean losing confidence in themselves and learning to trust in God. The path to greatness passes through failure and requires childlike humility and faith.

SOURCE MATERIAL

- Matthew 17:14-18:35

but not *just* more faith. They needed faith like a mustard seed. Mustard seeds are very small, but profoundly productive. Faith is like this too; even a small faith, if it is aimed at God, will produce great things. Here's the thing: a small amount of faith leads to prayer, and prayer shifts the responsibility to God. Think about the disciples' arrogance; they didn't even bother to pray for this demon to depart! The disciples thought that they could cast out demons without bothering God, but this kind only came out by prayer and fasting (Matt 17:21).

This was failure for the disciples, but it was a needed lesson. The path to glory goes through suffering, and failure is a kind of suffering. God had great things planned for the disciples—miracles much greater than casting out a demon—

Unit 4: Jesus Rejected

OBJECTIVES

Feel...

- peace about the possibility of failure; it is not something to fear.
- a sense of his need to become like a child.

Understand...

- that the disciples were unable to cast the demon out of the boy because they lacked faith and prayer.
- that, while failure is not good, fear of failure is not a reason to refrain from acting.
- that failure is a form of suffering that can lead to greater glory.
- that greatness in the kingdom is akin to childlike humility and faith.

Apply this understanding by...

- internalizing the truth that fear of failure should not keep us from acting.
- doing something good that you have avoided because of fear of failure.

---

but before they could have that greatness, they had to have faith.

As they continued, Jesus again reminded the disciples that He was going to suffer, die and be raised from the dead (Matt 17:22-23). He too had to go through suffering to find glory. Jesus was pointing them back to the way of the cross.

The narrative shifts at this point, but later we will see how this interaction would provoke a question from the disciples that would lead them back to the theme of suffering and glory. When they arrived at Capernaum, a tax collector for the temple tax came and asked Peter if Jesus paid the temple tax (Matt 17:24). Peter replied that He did. Shortly thereafter, Jesus talked to Peter about whether the temple tax was fair at all. After all, kings didn't tax their children; they taxed the people. Likewise, the children of the kingdom were sons of the King; therefore, they shouldn't be taxed either. Jesus didn't have any problem attacking ungodly institutions as He showed when He flipped tables at the temple. He would do the same again later. For now though, He paid the temple tax and left the argument alone, simply so He wouldn't cause offense; now was not the time or the place.

Jesus' talk of the children of the King provoked a question from the disciples. They asked, essentially, "If children of the King are great in the kingdom, who is greatest?" (Matt 18:1). In response, Jesus called a little child to Himself and set that child before the disciples. Jesus said, "Assuredly, I say to you, unless you are converted and become as little children, you will by no means enter the kingdom of heaven. Therefore whoever humbles himself as this little child is the greatest in the kingdom of heaven" (Matt 18:3-4).

Jesus was repeating, in a sense, the way of the cross. Jesus was teaching that the way to greatness is not an "onward and upward" kind of thing. The way to greatness requires becoming like little children. For the disciples, it meant humility, prayer, faith, and recognizing their need for the Father. This was the follow-up to their failure to heal the demonized boy. They thought that *they* could do it, when really they needed God to do it. They needed faith; they needed to pray. Spiritual growth is the inverse of what physical growth looks like; more spiritual maturity means you are more like a child. Greatness does not mean independence, but full dependence on God.

Then Jesus gave a warning. If those like children are the greatest in the kingdom of heaven, then those who mislead children are in big trouble. They are enemies of the kingdom, leading astray the ones Jesus came to save (Matt 18:6-7).

The remainder of Matthew 18 expands on the idea of relationships in the kingdom. Jesus came to save the lost, so how should the Church deal with those who go astray? In Matthew 18:15-19, Jesus describes the proper procedure to restore one who has gone astray within the Church. This is the foundational passage for Church discipline. The details of how this works are outside the scope of this lesson, but the basic point is that discipline is for restoration, not to drive the "sinners" out of the Church. With that in mind, the best way to restore a sinner is carefully and with time; that is the method laid out in Matthew 18.

As a follow-up question, Peter asked Jesus how many times he had to forgive his repentant brother. Thinking he was being generous, Peter asked, "Up to seven times?" (Matt 18:21). Jesus answered that there was no number—up to seventy times seven. Forgiveness (like faith) is the lifeblood of the Church. Jesus illustrated this truth with the parable of the unmerciful servant (Matt 18:23-35). The point here is that God has forgiven everyone in the kingdom more than any of us have had to forgive our brother; so in keeping with "Be perfect as your Father in heaven is perfect" (Matt 5:48), we should always forgive.

APPLICATION

Many people are afraid of failure, and this fear keeps them from action. Are you guilty of this? Has God called you to do something but you won't because you are afraid to fail? The application here is to be bold: share the gospel with an unbeliever or stand up for someone who is getting picked on. The path of discipleship *inevitably* passes through failure and in those failures is great potential for learning and growth. Follow Jesus by doing the one thing that you know is right but have been afraid to attempt because of the possibility of failure.

ACTIVITIES

1. Children and Greatness. Jesus taught that true greatness requires being like a child. Make a list of characteristics children have that Jesus might have had in mind.

Unit 4: Jesus Rejected

What are some practical ways you can live more like a child as Jesus taught? _____
_____
_____
_____

2. Journal Time: Fear of Failure. Spend some time writing in the space below about how the fear of failure can stop you from doing the things God wants you to do. Answer the following questions.

Why does fear of failure often stop us from doing what God wants us to do? _____
_____
_____

Why does God not want us to be afraid of failure? What are some things that we can learn through failure? _____
_____
_____

Write about something you are afraid of doing because you are afraid of failing. Ask God to give you the courage to do what He wants you to, even if you might fail at it. _____
_____
_____
_____
_____
_____
_____
_____
_____
_____
_____
_____

EVALUATION

1. Why were the disciples unable to cast the demon out of the boy who was brought to them? _____

2. Why is trying to do something good and failing better than not trying at all? _____

3. How is failure related to the way of the cross? In other words, why is failure found on the path to glory? _____

4. How is being like a child a good thing for a Christian? _____

www.ingramcontent.com/pod-product-compliance
Lightning Source LLC
Chambersburg PA
CBHW081337080526
44588CB00017B/2654